THE HEAD NEGRO IN CHARGE SYNDROME

Also by Norman Kelley

FICTION

Black Heat

The Big Mango

A Phat Death

NONFICTION

Rhythm & Business: The Political Economy of Black Music

THE HEAD NEGRO IN CHARGE SYNDROME

THE DEAD END OF BLACK POLITICS

NORMAN KELLEY

NATION BOOKS • NEW YORK

THE HEAD NEGRO IN CHARGE SYNDROME: The Dead End of Black Politics

Copyright © 2004 Norman Kelley

Published by Nation Books
An Imprint of Avalon Publishing Group
245 West 17th St., 11th Floor
New York, NY 10011

Nation Books is a co-publishing venture of the Nation Institute and Avalon Publishing Group Incorporated.

Library of Congress Cataloging-in-Publication Data
Kelley, Norman, 1954–
    The head Negro in charge syndrome:the death of Black politics/by Norman
Kelly.
        p. cm.
    Includes bibliographical references (p.) and index.
    ISBN 1-56025–584–6
    1. African Americans—Politics and government 2. African American leadership. 3. Political culture—United States. 4. United States—Race relations—Political aspects. 5. United States—Politics and government—1945–1989. 6. United States—Politics and government—1989–7. African Americans—Intellectual life. 8. African American
intellectuals. I. Title.

E185.615.K374 2004
324'.089'96073—dc22

2004046486

Book design by Paul Paddock
Printed in the United States of America
Distributed by Publishers Group West

INTRODUCTION
1

CHAPTER ONE
THE HEAD NEGRO IN CHARGE SYNDROME AND THE MAN
WHO WOULD BE JESSE (AKA SCAMPAIGN 2004)
21

CHAPTER TWO
FOLLOW THE LEADERS? THE DEATH OF EFFECTIVE
BLACK POLITICS
45

CHAPTER THREE
THE ROOTS OF SYMBOLIC POLITICS, 1965–1975: THE RISE AND
FALL OF BLACK POWER NATIONALISM
83

CHAPTER FOUR
THE POLITICS AND ECONOMICS OF SOUL POWER, OR "GOOD-
FOOT" CAPITALISM AND BLACK AMERICA'S RHYTHM NATION
117

CHAPTER FIVE
NOTES ON THE NIGGARATI—OR, WHY DEAD WHITE
MEN STILL RULE
137

CHAPTER SIX
THE POLITICS OF ELECTORAL INSTABILITY: BLACK VOTERS AND
STRATEGIC NON-VOTING
167

POSTSCRIPT:
SCAMPAIGN 2004
193

APPENDIX
PRESIDENT'S URBAN STRATEGY (CISNEROS MEMO)
199

TEN THINGS THAT COULD BE DONE
TO REVITALIZE BLACK POLITICS
213

NOTES
215

BIBLIOGRAPHY
227

A NOTE TO THE READERS
235

INDEX
237

Thus it is well to seem merciful, faithful, humane, sincere, religious and also be so; but you must have the mind so disposed that when it is needful to be otherwise you may be able to change to the opposite qualities. . . .

A prince must take great care that nothing goes out of his mouth which is not full of the above-named five qualities, and, to see and hear him, he should seem to be all mercy, faith, integrity, humanity and religion. And nothing is more necessary than to seem to have this last quality, for men in general judge more by eyes than by the hand, for every one can see, but very few have to feel. . . . Let a prince therefore aim at conquering and maintaining the state, and the means will always be judged honorable and praised by everyone, for the vulgar is always taken by appearances and the issue of the event; and the world consists only of the vulgar, and the few who are not vulgar are isolated when the many have a rallying point in the prince.

—Niccolo Machiavelli, *The Prince*

When you control a man's thinking you do not have to worry about his actions. You do not have to tell him not to stand here or go yonder. He will find his "proper place" and will stay in it. You do not need to send him to the back door. He will go without being told. In fact, if there is no back door, he will cut one out for his special benefit. His education makes it necessary.

—Carter G. Woodson, *Mis-education of the Negro*

INTRODUCTION

When Harvard president Lawrence Summers had a few choice words with Professor Cornel West regarding his activities at the country's most prestigious university, it was more than just a friendly chat. It was the bitch-slap heard 'round the world. Partly instigated by West's lame spoken-word CD, *Sketches of My Culture*, along with *allegations of* grade inflation, missing classes, advising Al Sharpton, and skating by on an exceedingly thin and unimpressive academic résumé, he was called into the woodshed. West, a rock star in the Lilliputian world of public intellectuals, took umbrage, called the president a cracker (in so many words by comparing him to Ariel Sharon), denounced his anti-affirmative action policy, and then decamped for his former place of employ, Princeton.

As a charter member of the post-1960s subdivision of the academic left's theoriocracy, the *niggarati*, West will probably be remembered for his role in *Matrix Reloaded* and *Matrix Revolutions* than for anything he has said or written. He's even been mentioned on the ABC series *The Practice*. In the words of one of his colleagues, however, "the man doesn't take risks" when it comes to substantive intellectual or political matters. Adolph Reed, perhaps his most astute critic, has said: "Cornel's work tends to be 1,000 miles wide and about two inches deep." Instead, West risks what little he has in attempting to be a rock star or wannabe hip-hop artist. It will be interesting to see if his role in *The Matrix* will be better remembered than Henry Louis Gates's recent appearance in an IBM commercial.

This is the *sad* state of black intellectualism in the early years of the twenty-first century: all posture, no substance. Today's black intellectuals are living examples of what the late social critic Neil Postman argued in *Amusing Ourselves to Death*: TV-like entertainment now dominates most, if not all, of the nation's social discourse and interaction. "Our politics, religion, news, athletics, education, commerce have been transformed into congenial adjuncts of show business, largely without protest or even popular notice," he wrote.[1]

Intellectuals, like political leaders, are now pop stars; where and how they appear in the medium is more important than what they actually write, think, or say.

In Russell Jacoby's 1987 book, *The Last Intellectuals* (which, to a degree, ricochets off Lewis Coser's 1965 *Men of Ideas*), he noted the last of an independent intelligentsia that wrote about public concerns for a general, educated, reading audience. What has taken its place, due to market forces, gentrification, suburbanization, and academic careerism, is an *academic* intelligentsia that writes for itself in obtuse scholarly journals in an even more obtuse and obscure language. West, however, went the other way: With the publication of *Race*

Matters, he became accessible, he became a *market* intellectual, the successor of the public intellectual, but for all the wrong reasons. A *New York Times* bestseller, *Race Matters* cemented, in the public's mind, West's position as a public intellectual. Although speaking in healing tones about race it said nothing of significance about race, which is why it made it to the *NYT* bestseller list. It seems that subsequent to that slim tome's *sotto voce* view about America's ur-problem, race, West became a pop star, seduced by celebrity and better known for being "Cornel West," a brand, than for any original thoughts or views, save, perhaps, *Prophesy Deliverance!*, *The American Evasion of Philosophy*, or *The Ethical Dimensions of Marxist Thought*.[2]

If one wants to see a powerful mind at work, one could do no better than to read *Prophesy Deliverance!* West basically argues for an amalgamation of black theology (the "prophetic" tradition of the black church) and progressive Marxism (e.g., Antonio Gramsci, Theodor Adorno, Stanley Aronowitz, and others), since both of them have a tradition of questioning the status quo of white supremacy and capitalism, respectively. He sets off by investigating the "genealogy of modern racism," the European Enlightenment (the "structure of modern discourse"). By this he means the "controlling metaphors, notions, categories, and norms that shape the predominant conceptions of truth and knowledge in the modern west,"[3] which have lent themselves to power, classification, and domination of nature and other humans through science and commerce. Yet he says nothing in regard to those very same things—controlling metaphors, notions, categories, and norms—that came out of the *Christian* discourse and social tradition that rationalized and justified slavery and racism. For example, the curse of Ham (bestowed upon Ham by his drunk father, Noah, because Ham saw him naked)[4] that justified the enslavement of black people who were supposedly a "Hamitic" people, descendant of Ham. Or the papal bull of 1455 (*Romanus Pontifex*) by Pope Nicholas V, which licensed, so to speak, European explorers to enslave and Christianized "pagans" in Africa and the New World. And there's the classic: Paul admonishing slaves to "obey" their masters,[4] which surely warmed the cockles of the hearts of the master class while they ignored his stricture to them to treat slaves "justly and fairly."[5]

West spends a great deal of time preaching about black theologians questioning white racism, but he makes only one passing reference to the "countless calamities perpetrated by Christian churches."[6] He talks about the "genealogy" of modern European discourse's complicity with racism, but neglects to mention that Christianity is a precursor, along with Greek philosophy, of modern philosophy. In other words, the roots of modern racism have their antecedents in Christian practices and theology. Christian practice vis-á-vis blacks was simultaneously a religion of dominance *and* deliverance. He dodges that issue because black theology or African American religious tradition comes out of a theological *discourse* that has been used *against* black people, root and branch. While one can make an argument that blacks "dialectically" overcame the oppressive use of the Scriptures to forge a new Christianity, not to even address it underscores how much the book is a theoretical wish-fulfillment that has nothing to do with the history of the black church and blacks' relationship to Christianity. West ignores the dominance but concentrates on the deliverance. That is not what one would think a critical inquiry would do.

One should credit the black church with helping slaves adjust to the African slave trade. One should, however, also recognize, as did E. Franklin Frazier in *Black Bourgeoisie*, that Christianity was utilized to stamp a feeling of "natural inferiority" upon blacks, to "prove and give divine sanction" to blacks' alleged racial inferiority, and to justify their "exclusion from the races of mankind."[7] Genovese, however, argues that Christianity allowed the slaves to forge "weapons of defense, the most important of which was a religion that taught them to love and value each other, to take a critical view of their masters, and to reject the ideological rationales their own enslavement."[8]

One also has to understand that the legacy of the black church has hardly been progressive. While it did help blacks weather the storms of slavery and postslavery racism, it also hindered them from developing a modern outlook and keeps some of them locked in a religious provincialism (victimized by hucksters), allowing a patriarchal authoritarianism to take root along with a hostility to ideas and other means of self-assertion that was wasn't even challenged until the civil rights era.

Today the black church has slipped back into a pre–civil rights quietism. (Its conservative social base is exactly the sort that white conservatives seek to exploit against homosexuals. Of course these white conservatives are the same people who were oppressing blacks in the South.) Despite West's emphasis on black liberation theology and the prophetic tradition,

Calhoun-Brown noted that most of today's black clergy ignore such a "social gospel of reform and revolution."[9]

What is interesting is that West's rise as a pop star also mirrors the rise of *market* intellectuals en masse: academics who basically conform to the dictates of the media marketplace to perform roles as "experts" in a specialization. In West's case, like other black intellectuals, it's about being an "authentic" intellectual voice of black America. Because of an intellectually *phat* sounding lexicon he appeals to some whites who secretly suspect most blacks are not as intelligent as they. Thus he can be cited at cocktail parties as an "authority" on some afro-specific subject. For some blacks, however, he gives the appearance of being an "engaged" intellectual/activist even though most have probably never read a significant work by him; he affirms a black need to be thought of as intelligent without having to do the work that intelligence requires. Instead, he "performs" as an intellectual and in an anti-intellectual society like the United States, performance and style—emotional appeal—outweighs the intellect, the rational, and ideas.[10] The supreme irony, however, is that West's effect is less intellectual and more visceral. Because American society is both anti-intellectual and status-conscious, it covets the "expertise" indicated by those three letters behind his name while simultaneously scorning depth of knowledge.

West's appearance as a pop intellectual also mirrors the rise and fall of black America, which also occurred as the liberal, Democratic New Deal/New Frontier/Great Society regimes of Roosevelt, Kennedy and Johnson began to lose favor, attacked by a resurgent conservative movement. *Black America* rose in the "We Shall Overcome" days of the King years, the civil rights and black liberation struggles, but it essentially died in the 1980s when the Republican *risorgimento* rolled into Washington during the Reagan-Bush years. At a critical moment the established black leadership—the NAACP, the Congressional Black Caucus, intellectuals, essentially the black national political directorate—had no strategy to deal with the Republican assault on civil rights issues, and could not devise an agenda *beyond* civil rights. The black national political directorate had unilaterally disarmed itself during the 1970s when it went from "protest to politics," allowing the black vote to be incorporated into the Democratic Party—without the threat of sanctions or having an independent base. African Americans have no intellectual defense or programmatic offense because the people who are in the social position to think, ostensibly intellectuals, are more interested in being glib celebrities or critiquing what *is* and what *ain't* in hip-hop. A good example is Michael Eric Dyson, who is better known for being a "rapping" professor than for any alleged critical insight. It's about performance, not knowledge.

•   •   •

Essentially at this point in time and history black America is leaderless, drifting. This would not be an entirely unfortunate circumstance if it weren't for the development of a pernicious syndrome, the Head Negro in Charge (HNIC) Syndrome. This is a condition in which self-appointed "leaders" hijack the political process by somehow appealing to blacks' sense of collectivity, while having an agenda that is mostly about themselves, making *themselves* the leader. This syndrome and black political demobilization have been aided, as I have suggested, by a black intelligentsia that has become more obsessed with pop culture and celebrity. This has allowed its conservative wing to bloom and grow, and bum rush the policy debate over such issues as affirmative action, education, civil rights, voting, etc. These black conservatives are better at being public intellectuals than so-called oppositional intellectuals like West, bell hooks, Dyson, and others. These left-of-center intellectuals may purportedly speak to a public about public concerns, but it has been the black conservatives or neoconservatives— Thomas Sowell, Shelby Steele, Glenn Loury, James McWhorter, Armstrong Williams and others—who influence public debate about public policy issues.

West is emblematic of a trend: African American market intellectuals who profit while they prophet, selling attitude. The common practice is to do some supposedly serious work, and then dispense wisdom on subjects like hope, love, and self-esteem, or write hagiographies on King or Tupac Shakur or hip-hop. In other words, kitsch, or, since such work tends to be aimed at blacks, *afro-kitsch*. This has meant African American political culture has surrendered the field of public policy to black conservatives, aided and abetted by the mainstream (white) conservative movement, to set the parameters of debate on important social, political, and economic questions. It is left to nonstar academics to produce such works as *Whitewashing Race: The Myth of a Color-blind Society*. Produced by a team of scholars—Michael K. Brown, Martin Carnoy, Elliot Currie, Troy Duster, David Oppenheimer, Majorie M. Shultz, and David Wellman—it challenges the conservative claims that racism is a thing of past and that today's racial inequalities have more to do with individual black failures. Their work begs the question: Why didn't West or Henry Louis Gates, the director of the black studies department at Harvard, initiate such a project? Instead they have offered coffee-table books like *The African American Century*, an updated version of great moments in Negro history.

The central theme of this book is the "disappearance" or devolution of black leadership and its role in African American political demobilization in the past thirty years. By "disappearance" I mean that black leadership—elected officials, civil rights leaders, and intellectuals—and black politics no longer function as a means to the end of creating the conditions under which black Americans might enjoy material, cultural, and social equality with white Americans. The inability to do so— in effect, the inability to solve problems—has led to the rise of "symbolic politicians," HNICs who aspire to the pretense of leadership without being accountable or presenting solutions. Head Negroes are counterparts of the *postmodern princes* (or master politicans), usually white politicians very good at using images and artifice: John Kennedy, Richard Nixon, George Wallace, Ronald Reagan, Newt Gingrich, Bill Clinton, and now George W. Bush. The major difference, however, is that a postmodern prince actually achieves power. HNICs excel at "symbolic action," as evidenced by Louis Farrakhan, who initiated the so-called Million Man March, or Jesse Jackson's and Al Sharpton's presidential runs. They can rabble-rouse but can't effectively lead for sustained periods, and they are certainly not interested in rethinking old ideas or building institutions for subsequent generations. They are hustlers *par excellence*, born and bred in a United States of con artists, sharpies, and requisite suckers. Elected black officials, likewise, have pretty much retreated from effective leadership. Most of today's black politics, electoral and nonelectoral, is symbolic.

A good example is the "reparations movement," which appeals to some blacks emotionally because black leaders have failed them so miserably in such matters as economic development, crime, education, etc. While African Americans are *morally* entitled to reparations, that doesn't necessarily mean that they will receive it or should spend a great deal of time chasing after it. (Besides, how does one financially quantify what some call the African holocaust?) Some members of the black elite, like lawyers and historians scrutinizing corporate records, would rather do that than confront the implosion of public education that affects lower-income black and Latino children. Merely following through on some of the recommendations in this book's appendix, particularly using information technologies to hotwire public housing complexes or to seed inner cities as a "network of electronic villages," would do vastly more than organizing for an elusive pot of gold. One gets the impression that the black elite is doing this because the said issue has bubbled up from the grassroots and is a cheap emotional way to show symbolic "leadership" and intraracial solidarity—a way to make up for past leadership failings. (See appendix.)

Another example is what happened after the Million Man March. A biracial, bipartisan group of U.S. representatives urged President Clinton to establish a bipartisan commission to study race relations in the United States. Of the group were Charles Rangel (D-NY), who had attended the march, John Lewis (D-GA), and Eleanor Holmes Norton (Del.-D.C.)—all black, all members of the Congressional Black Caucus (CBC). As always, blacks were supplicants approaching a president who had been as cynical in his dealings with them as the GOP has been while using its neo-racist tactics over the past thirty years or more. Nothing could be more evidentiary as to the total irrelevancy and political and intellectual bankruptcy of black leadership. Surprisingly, the CBC never thought about rallying *their* constituents for a march on Washington to challenge the not too undisclosed war on blacks codified in the GOP's "Contract with America." Their failure to do so was a sign of the total absence of effective black political action. (Clinton, by the way, did not establish such a commission until his *last* year in office.) The black political class refuses to deal with a reality that the vast majority of blacks understand only too well: that integration has been a questionable enterprise when it comes to *power* and that blacks, regardless of class, are vulnerable because they lack *economic* as well as political power.

Perhaps nothing better symbolized the calculating co-optation, the utter capitulation of black politics than Bill Clinton's summer 1998 Martha's Vineyard appearance in the "colored" section of that vacation retreat. Clinton was on the ropes after he finally admitted to having an affair with the zaftig Monica Lewinsky. The president, unquestionably

America's greatest politician, in the narrowest sense of the word, was able to survive the impeachment imbroglio because of his mastery of divide-and-conquer identity politics: all symbolism, no substance.

What did he do?

Clinton did a James Brown. The Godfather's most cherished routine was to sing "Please, Please, Please" with such fervor that he would drop to his knees, begging. Then one of the Flames—a backup singer—would drape a cape around him and lead him away from the microphone, consoling him. Suddenly, the hardest-working man in show business would break away, return to the microphone, and engage in another round of soul-stirring pyrotechnics.

Clinton's James Brown performance took place before 400 people in Oak Bluffs, Massachusetts, in a simple wood-shingled chapel on Martha's Vineyard. This selection of the elect had gathered to celebrate one of the seminal events in American history, the civil rights movement's 1963 March on Washington. Clinton gave a speech and read from former civil rights activist and now Congressman John Lewis's memoir *Walking With the Wind*. Then he held hands with others and sang "We Shall Overcome"—his version of "Please, Please, Please." Charles J. Ogletree, a Harvard Law professor, Henry Louis Gates Jr., another member of the Harvard faculty, and Anita Hill were also there. Ogletree supported the president for several reasons: minority appointments to the Cabinet, judgeships, Clinton's visit to Africa and the President's Initiative on Race. The unmistakable genius of the Clinton administration was that it could buy blacks so cheap (although the conservative movement can purchase black conservative endorsement of its policies for even less).

Clinton's success in confusing black voters convinced black elected officials and so-called black public intellectuals to do even less than usual. It's well known that Clinton was, and still is, popular with black voters because he had learned how to finesse America's racial politics with his deft way of not appearing anti-black while engaging in coded anti-black politics (on crime, welfare, etc.).

Black politics and black political culture regressed during the age of Clinton. Once there was a King exhorting the nation to live up to its democratic precepts, a Malcolm X eviscerating America's racial policies, an Adam Clayton Powell legislating an array of laws that affected American public policy, and, even more important, black popular mobilization. Louis Farrakhan and the then-new nigga white America loved to hate, the late Khalid Muhammad, seemed to be striking a chord with some blacks—or to be filling a political vacuum. Neither Farrakhan nor Muhammad had anything substantial to offer, yet they understood one essential thing about black politics: It feeds off symbols. They understood they would pay no political price for not delivering the goods, as is the tendency in today's black politics. It's equivalent to Homer Simpson bellowing, "Suckers!"

The state of affairs of African American political leadership stems from the fact that it follows a broker-agent model: Usually, charismatic black individuals claim to represent the black community as a whole before institutional policymakers. The pre-eminent example of such is Jesse Jackson, a man who garnered black (and white) votes in 1984 and 1988 and traded them for positions that strengthened him as an interest-group power broker, a position that rarely benefits the greatest number of average blacks. Now blacks have the Rev. Al Sharpton doing a "Jesse."

The black intelligentsia apparently had no interest in pointing out the glaring contradictions between Clinton's symbolic politics and his antiblack politics, except, perhaps, Adolph Reed. Instead, Toni Morrison and Manning Marable discoursed on Clinton's "blackness," or the tropes of such, but one did not hear a single *J'accuse*! from them, which affirmed Harold Cruse's condemnation of the black intellectual class as a "colossal fraud." This pass was made possible by the "fact" that Clinton was seen—touted—as the "first black President," a hybrid assertion that has garnered even more currency and idiocy in the apolitical age of hip hop, where whites can affect blackness but not have to pay the social cost of actually being black in America. This is the unintended consequence of black power's cultural-nationalist variant that stressed cultural forms over substance. If one believes in Kwanzaa and Afrocentricity, why not that Clinton is "black" in style? Hence no reason to extract concession; the First Brother is one of "us."

Weeks after the Martha's Vineyard showcase, Clinton and Al Gore appeared at the Congressional Black Caucus's annual weekend gathering in Washington and did a Sam and Dave version of "I Thank You." There, Gore ran down a list of black appointments that his boss had made to various departments: Energy, Agriculture, Commerce, Veterans Affairs, and Labor.

"As the list rolled on . . ." wrote Katharine Seelye of the *New York Times*, "its sheer length and Mr. Gore's full throttle rendition brought the audience to its feet with sustained applause."[11]

Missing from that list were the other ways in which Clinton had tended to the needs of African Americans and served the larger cause of justice. He fired Surgeon General Joycelyn Elders; shoved aside his Justice Department candidate and friend Lani Guinier; affirmed the execution of a mentally defective black Arkansas inmate; signed a horrific crime bill that restricted *habeas corpus* but widened the scope of wiretapping and added new federal death penalty provisions; refused to equalize the disparity between crack and powder cocaine sentencing, so that blacks continue getting hit the hardest over the former; signed the egregious welfare reform bill; signed NAFTA; and disallowed the use of the word "genocide" in reports, knowing full well that doing so would prohibit an American response to the genocidal killings in Rwanda. Moreover, he did not say or do anything about the rampant rise of police brutality in cities with sizable black populations.

And this is precisely the problem. Really intractable problems like police brutality, racial profiling, and crumbling public schools are given short shrift. But Clinton's symbolic politics underscored the class schisms in black America. While those at Oak Bluffs and at the CBC black-tie chowdown are moving on up, those who earn $50,000 or less are facing a political system that has openly become a plutocracy, aided and abetted by putative black leadership, politicos, and public intellectuals.

There's Charles Rangel, a New York City Democrat, smitten with the idea of Hillary Clinton running for Senate from New York, telling her that she didn't even have to worry about submitting to a primary! An untested novice with considerable political baggage was given the nomination without any competition or prior review by the electorate. Why? Because she's the wife of the party's chief fundraiser! Very democratic.

Then there's the Confederate flag issue (an emblem of treasonous losers, no doubt). As odious as the Stars and Bars are, it doesn't rank with immediate problems for blacks, like crumbling school systems, racial profiling, dwindling jobs. *As with the issue of reparations*, black organizations like the NAACP would prefer to deal with the flag issue rather than the collapse of public education. It's understandable. Black Leadership, Inc. is simply a business, another industry. And because of the false politics of race in the country, programs like affirmative action become a way for some blacks on either side of the political spectrum to gain points. Black Leadership, Inc. has made a tacit agreement, as argued by Michael Lind in *The Next American Nation*, not to disrupt the status quo—a status quo that benefits it. The grand compromise of multicultural America is the tacit understanding between the white overclass and the nonwhite overclass that in return for being granted benefits in the form of "racial preference" programs for middle- and upper-class African Americans, black and Hispanic leaders will not engage in disruptive mass agitation like that of the '60s.

Thus, there is no popular mobilization now because a

segment of the black population—liberal and conservative—has become aligned with the white overclass. The fix is in, and black leadership, as it has been formally constituted, no longer exists. The current crop of so-called black leaders and intellectuals recalls Frantz Fanon's prescient view regarding the corrupt nature of the postcolonial African bourgeoisie: "Its innermost vocation seems to be to keep in the running and to be part of the racket."

Today black elected leaders are a *comprador* class, i.e., intermediaries whose sole function is to channel black votes into the Democratic Party apparatus while the party ignores black needs and gears its programs to white suburban voters or Reagan Democrats. It throws a bone to blacks with affirmative action, but that program has a tendency to affect those who already have means. Senator Trent Lott's exuberant nostalgia for Senator Strom Thurmond's discredited segregationist platform merely underscored how the Republicans have been in denial about their neo-racist political shenanigans for the past thirty years or more. After all, the 1964 election initiated white Southern Democrats becoming members of the GOP via the "Southern strategy." (The revelation that Thurmond had an illegitimate child with his family's black maid, however, underscores the wit and wisdom of Alabama's Governor "Big" Jim Folsom. He observed that while white folks would get worked up about segregation during the day, there would be "a whole lot of integratin' goin' on at night."[12])

This book will argue that this disappearance, or devolution, of black leadership can be traced to a series of assumptions that civil rights leaders made about the connection between politics and economics. They assumed that the end of state-sanctioned segregation and discrimination would set in motion events that would lead to economic parity between blacks and whites. It did not. While there has been progress in the status of African Americans, a third are mired in poverty not solely because of their "culture of poverty" but because of the systemic function of race, politics, and economics. When the civil rights acts of the 1960s were passed, some in the movement argued that it was now time to go from protest to politics, eschewing direct action, and building electoral coalitions. This was necessary in order to implement the next phase of the civil rights movement: "economic justice." However, *The HNIC Syndrome* argues that by de-linking direct action (or not having an independent political organization) from policy implementation, black politics, as practiced within the confines of American political system, has been rendered ineffective. Blacks are taken for granted by the Democrats and ignored by the Republicans. Black leaders never sought to engage in "internal development" in the inner cities and poverty-stricken rural enclaves, or even thought about how to go about doing so.

Instead, we have symbolic political leaders: Jackson, Farrakhan, and Sharpton. These are charismatic "race men" who do not care a whit about real policies that improve the life chances of African Americans.

While Jackson may have initially engaged in "progressive" politics by going out to the heartland in the 1980s to promote a version of black-and-white-unite-and-fight, he was primarily motivated, like all politicians, by the psychopathology of power. In Jackson's case, he rationalized *his* primary agenda—recognition and power—into a progressive movement, and his previous association with King—although King himself was wary of Jackson's naked ambition[13]—allowed him to become the heir apparent of progressive politics, black and white. He has never really posed a serious wealth-redistributive threat to the status quo—as evidenced by his Wall Street Project, which has cynically appropriated King's legacy as a cover for Jackson's crony capitalism. And to a degree, he has impeded the development of any progressive black movement for almost twenty years. His example and "success" have set an example for the likes of Louis Farrakhan and The Man Who Would Be Jesse, Al Sharpton. Despite Kenneth Timmerman's claim in *Shakedown: Exposing the Real Jesse Jackson* that Jackson was a "tool of the left," it was essentially the other way around: He used the left as a means to bolster his two egocentric presidential campaigns. He should be given credit by the right for thwarting any real left-of-center third-party formation and for helping the rise of the right's favorite *bête blanc*, Bill Clinton.

• • •

For years some, including myself, have wondered why it is that black politics has become so dismal, cynical, corrupt, and ineffective despite there being more blacks in political office and at prestigious universities. Why have blacks allowed others to act in their name? Why do we not hold these people accountable? Is it just about blackness or is it also about the results of social and public policies that affect blacks and all Americans? *The Head Negro in Charge Syndrome* will attempt to present an analysis of an interesting chapter in African American political culture, calling, as one proud Negro demands, for "the reinvigoration of black political ideas."[14]

This book begins with a topology of the rise of the HNIC syndrome and melds into the man who would be Jesse: Al Sharpton and his "Scampaign." Chapter one also examines the man who has made a cottage industry of symbolic politics in black America, Louis Farrakhan. Chapters two and three, respectively, will examine the history of the decline of effective black politics in the civil rights era and the roots of symbolic politics in Black Power. Shifting gears, chapter four looks at James Brown—that's right, JB!—and tries to situate him in the political economy of black music in the 1960s struggles. Chapter five examines the role of the niggarati, left-of-center black intellectuals, and will argue that it's the ideas of Dead White Men that rule while the members of the niggarati are posing as public intellectuals. Chapter six ends with an argument for blacks to reconsider their relationship to the Democratic Party and consider the politics of electoral instability.

CHAPTER ONE

THE HEAD NEGRO IN CHARGE SYNDROME AND THE MAN WHO WOULD BE JESSE
(AKA SCAMPAIGN 2004)

The Head Negro in Charge Syndrome has its roots originally in white domination over blacks and the selection of certain blacks to be in control of others, especially the "head nigra" controlling the labor of the other blacks on the plantations. However, this syndrome can also be traced to the oral and religious traditions of African Americans, with the preacher as the intermediary between white power and the black masses. As W. E. B. Du Bois once observed in *The Souls of Black Folk:*

> The preacher is the most unique personality developed by the Negro on American soil. A leader, a politician, an orator, a "boss," an intriguer, an idealist—all these he is, and ever, too, the center of a group of men, now twenty, now a thousand in number. The combination of certain adroitness with deep-seated earnestness, of tact with consummate ability, gave him his preeminence, and helps him to maintain it. The type, of course, varies according to time and place . . .[1]

Black political culture tends to be charismatic, meaning that leadership is bestowed upon the individual possessing special gifts of the body or the spirit. In black America, the man (and it usually is a man) who can dynamically and expressively denote the mood or the will of the Africans in America becomes a leader, but not through democratic means. Yet this tendency has a major drawback: Charismatic leadership generally does not build or establish permanent institutions or institutionalize daily practices like thinking or follow-through. Charismatic leaders are men of the moment, usually a moment of great distress. When they leave, however, they do not leave behind patterns and practices that can be sustained over generations. Thus, today, black America tends to be *organizationally* weak as the result of its political culture being charismatically drenched by such leaders as King, Malcolm X, Jesse Jackson, Louis Farrakhan, and pseudo-charismatic, like Al Sharpton. None of these men have left behind or engendered strong organizations.

This aspect of black political culture is so prevalent that even some brilliant minds fail to detect it. For example, while on a "Pass the Mic" tour, which featured Tavis Smiley, Cornel West, and Michael Eric Dyson, a radio phone-in caller on WNYC's *Brian Lehrer Show* raised the question why Al Sharpton did not have a stronger organization in the pre-election campaign.[2] The general consensus, after all three expressed their "love" and admiration for the reverend, was that Sharpton was the victim of a series of actions for which he couldn't be entirely held accountable—meaning Jesse Jackson not leaving behind a strong organizational legacy and the general state of black leadership. Most interesting, however, is that Dyson had earlier mentioned how Sharpton's style and rhetorical flair stem from the black church. Yet not one of the three thought that this may have been the problem: that black political leaders—once again, charismatics from the black church tradition—tend not to establish strong organizational mechanisms to ensure a continuance of political efforts or the promotion of ideas beyond the political season. That neither West nor Dyson, supposedly "two of America's most important social thinkers," experts on black affairs and culture, as touted by Smiley himself, failed to acknowledge or even recognize this tendency of African American political culture says a great deal.

Yet one Dead White Male provides some insight into "charismatic authority":

> In contrast to any kind of bureaucratic organization of offices, the charismatic structure knows nothing of a form or an ordered procedure of appointment or dismissal. It knows no regulated "career," "advancement," "salary," or regulated and expert training of the holder of charisma or of his aids. It knows no agency of control or appeal, no local bailiwicks or exclusive functional jurisdictions; nor does it embrace permanent institutions like our bureaucratic "departments," which are independent of persons and of purely personal charisma.[3]

Interestingly, another scholar's view echoes that above,

but it is about black charismatic authority and the black church. He wrote:

> [T]he major organizations among black Americans, the Christian churches, followed a polity farthest removed from modern bureaucratic and hierarchical forms of organization. In this sense, the organizational form of most Afro-American churches, charismatic and often autocratic in leadership, neither promoted nor encouraged widespread respect for and acquisition of bureaucratic skills requisite for accountable leadership and institutional longevity. In short, the Christian churches' organizational form imposed constraints on the administrative capabilities and institutional capacities of black people.[4]

The first passage was from Max Weber, renowned German sociologist, famous for *The Protestant Ethic and the Spirit of Capitalism*; the second passage is from Cornel West's own book, *Prophesy Deliverance!*, which he apparently doesn't remember writing.

The most powerful example of the HNICS is the post–Civil War, post-Reconstruction rise of nonpreacher Booker T. Washington, "the wizard of Tuskegee," whose famed speech at the 1895 Atlanta Exposition before a white audience skyrocketed him to the role of Responsible Negro Leader. He is also the patron saint of black conservatism. Washington's speech was called the "Atlanta compromise" by other blacks who felt he had compromised blacks' basic democratic and social rights as American citizens. It set the tone and mode for the politics of white ordination of black leadership and was the essential mode of control over the "Negro problem" before the civil rights movement. It also became a route by which some blacks could gain access and privilege by telling whites what they wanted to hear, much in the way that some of today's black conservatives serve as "pet Negroes" by rationalizing conservative policies that run counter to the interests of a larger number of blacks. Conservatives, generally, are interested in power, not theory, and black conservatives tend to provide rationalizations for Republican domestic policies. However, with Condoleezza Rice as George W. Bush's National Security Adviser and Colin Powell as his Secretary of State, we're now witnessing black conservatives providing the same kind of services for policies in the international field.[5]

Back in the day, however, Responsible Negro Leaders were picked, encouraged, and fêted by whites, especially during the formation of the post–Civil War African American political culture, with Negro ministers and educators like Washington at the fulcrum of this politics: compromised, cautious, authoritarian, and anti-intellectual. With the passing of Washington and the eclipse of the "Tuskegee" machine, which was a patronage apparatus that dictated the appointment of blacks to political office, and with blacks moving north and acquiring education and greater economic opportunity, the role of the unelected Head Negro spokesman became untenable. But in all fairness, one must admit that Washington, as a secular leader, did manage to leave behind a school and a problematic legacy.

Marcus Garvey, another charismatic, could also be placed in the category of secular leader. His United Negro Improvement Association tapped into the deep reservoir of black nationalism that rose in the post–World War I years, making him the sort of troublesome Negro that provoked the ire of other blacks and the federal government. Garvey's greatest transgression may well be the fact that he was not "pre-approved" by whites as the right sort of Negro leader. To some native-born American blacks, also, he had become a race leader over *their* heads. Garvey was convicted of mail fraud, jailed, and then deported. Whatever his shortcomings, though, he set the tone for being a "race man," and established the sociological and political fact that black nationalism could be a potent organizing project to mere integration. However the UNIA did not survive, only the idea of black unity.

Yet after the passing of Garvey from the scene some of black America's best-known "race men" and leaders have tended to be ministers: Adam Clayton Powell Jr., Martin Luther King Jr., Elijah Muhammad, Malcolm X, Jesse Jackson, Louis Farrakhan, and Al Sharpton. Some of these men are part of black political culture's HNIC Syndrome, which has a sub-part: the M&M complex, short for Messiah & Massa, a mixture of psychological and political group dynamics that are played out within black culture and the broader American culture.

In the Messiah complex, based on both Mosaic and Chris-tological symbolism, an indispensable, usually charismatic black leader is seen as a deliverer or redeemer. This leader shows his people to the promised land, or exhorts them to live up to their potential, or challenges whites to honor the promises of American democracy, reminding the nation of its shortcomings. The best examples are such charismatics as Garvey, King, Elijah Muhammad, Malcolm X, Jackson, Farrakhan, and Sharpton. There have been lesser examples: Father Divine, Daddy Grace, and Reverend Ike, whose saying "One of the best things you can do for the poor is not be one of them" displays the mercenary thrust of his ministry. And it should be noted that there is a strong martyrdom tradition within African American political culture because of the fact that some of their leaders and benefactors have often been assassinated. Today the martyrdom tradition has passed from political leaders to hip-hop artists, most notably Tupac Shakur. This also may have historical implications insofar as some aspects of black political culture have a tendency to respond to the "strong leader" (or "strong black man"), which may have roots in African political formations before European domination.

The Massa complex, however, based on blacks' psychopolitical needs, is best exemplified by such national leaders as Abraham Lincoln, FDR, John Kennedy, Robert Kennedy, and, now, Bill Clinton. Usually such white men are seen as sympathetic figures (a residue of white paternalism internalized by blacks), having bestowed some benefit on blacks or having displayed other than hostile interest in their situation. Unsophisticated blacks have a tendency to interpret such behavior as benevolence when it has been, in fact, most likely based on political calculation, having very little to do with respecting blacks as legitimate members of the body politic. Also, blacks know who has the real power, and it usually isn't them since they still continue to organize to achieve it; meanwhile they defer to such whites while sounding black, proud, and determined. This is why some could attend Farrakhan's rally one day yet make a beeline a day or so later to the White House to ask for a commission on race. Blacks have a tendency to be loyal to a fault. They remained loyal to the Republican Party even after it betrayed them during the compromise of 1877, which afterward ushered in Jim Crow terrorism and political disenfranchisement that wasn't toppled until the civil rights era. Blacks loved the Kennedys, but often these Irish-American Brahmins were quite cynical in dealing with them, as accounts by Taylor Branch[6] and Thomas Reeves[7] showed. During the 1960s and 1970s it wasn't uncommon to find a kitsch troika of the slain Kennedy brothers and MLK adorning the walls of many black households.

No better contemporary example of the Massa complex can be found than the relationship that Bill Clinton has with blacks despite his record of soft-coded racial usage at the expense of blacks. A pathetic example of this complex ran in a November 2003 *New York Times* article, "An Open Message for Bill Clinton: Your Neighbors in Harlem Miss You Like Crazy."[8] In the story the denizens of the most famous black enclave in the world bemoaned not seeing the "First Brother"; he wasn't around to assist them with their personal problems or the issues confronting Harlem. Needless to say, Clinton was traversing the world and the country, taking care of *his* business. Clinton has been able to achieve this unjustified admiration because of this aspect of black political culture, but he is also a superb postmodern prince who knows how to play to some blacks' need for recognition from whites. This doesn't mean that blacks slavishly follow the dictates of whites, for blacks have evolved beyond that. What it does mean, however, is that some blacks have a need, a desire for recognition or validation from whites, and some whites know how to play those chords. (If one wants an example of how Clinton avoided addressing the concerns of blacks, see the appendix: "President's Urban Strategy.")

If it can be argued that blacks have had a prophetic tradition, speaking truth to power, it can also be argued that the same tradition has led them to prophetic accommodation with white power.

However, the most recent version of the Head Negro in Charge tends to be a self-appointed, rather than white selected, mountebank with an agenda that is masked as representing the collective interests of blacks under the notion of "a seat at the table." No real organizing or mobilization takes place. In other words, *individual interests as racial brokerage*. What makes this new-jack version of the HNIC very interesting is that blacks already have people to represent them: elected officials. Yet black political representation during the past thirty years has been so feeble and compromised that these self-appointed leaders have been able to rise to the top in post–civil rights black political culture.

Such is the case of Al Sharpton and Louis Farrakhan.

SCAMPAIGN 2004

"I'm qualified, probably more qualified than any other person who is expected to be on the Democratic ticket for 2004, because I actually have a following and I speak for the people," boasted the Rev. Al Sharpton in 2003. Sharpton was in preparation for his campaign to secure the 2004 Democratic presidential nomination, a campaign that had all the markings of a Jesse Jackson redux.

The prize for Sharpton, of course, is to become the third Head Negro in Charge (HNIC). This syndrome has witnessed the rise of symbolic leaders—Jesse Jackson, Louis Farrakhan, Sharpton, and potentially Russell Simmons—who may be charismatic, but are politically unaccountable to the very people they claim to represent, namely African Americans. This transformation has been underway since the 1970s, but most African Americans have yet to confront it. Because black America has not faced up to the moribund nature of black politics, it has witnessed the rise of these symbolic leaders.

And yet Sharpton's candidacy, in the eyes of some, does have its virtues.

"Compared to some of the other candidates in the race, he's just as qualified," said David Bositis, senior researcher of the Joint Center for Political and Economic Studies, a black-oriented think tank. "But he's not going to get the nomination."

But because the black vote is important to Democrats, Bositis thinks Sharpton could force the major candidates to confront topics that might otherwise be ignored. These include issues of economic justice, a whole variety of criminal-justice issues and low-income housing. A similar rationale is offered by the candidate himself: "Even if I lo se," Sharpton has said, "I have the option to negotiate points with the Democratic Party."

Like Jackson, Sharpton may also be compelling enough to convince young blacks to vote when they otherwise might not. And they "may stick around to vote some more," argued Bositis.

Some in big media have already dismissed Sharpton as a joke and a nuisance. Handicapping the 2004 Democratic aspirants on public radio, *Time* columnist Joe Klein called Sharpton "a criminal, a buffoon, and a waste of time."

Others, like Robert C. Smith, professor of political science at San Francisco State University and author of *We Have No Leaders: African Americans in the Post—Civil Rights Era*, while not as hostile, are still less optimistic about Sharpton's agenda. "I think [his candicacy] is a mistake," said Smith. "I don't think he can achieve any of the objectives he's laid out for himself in the campaign." Smith is one of a number of black political theorists who view today's generation of black leaders as functionally "irrelevant." This is due to their inability to "mobilize the limited resources of the Black community as part of a strategy and program to extract from society the resources necessary to reconstruct urban African American communities," Smith (with co-author Ronald Walters) wrote in *African American Leadership*.

Smith, who calls himself a "strong supporter" of Jackson's two forays into electoral politics in the 1980s, sees the objectives of Sharpton's and Jackson's campaigns as identical. "Hardly any of [Jackson's] objectives were achieved," continued Smith, who believes Jackson's two presidential bids unintentionally moved the Democratic Party to the right. With the party losing in 1980, 1984, and 1988 with liberal white candidates, the more conservative wing wasn't going to countenance an insurgent black voice that alienated white voters. Smith thinks Sharpton may have similar unintended consequences on top of failing to broaden the Democratic base or nudge the party leftward—and Republicans are smiling at the prospect. "I can't see anything for black leadership or the black community that will be served by his candidacy," argued the professor. "I think the only thing it will do is what Jackson's candidacy did, which is . . . to enhance his status as a national leader. [This is] one of Sharpton's principal objectives."

This is HNIC Syndrome, in which maverick presidential campaigns and Million Man March (MMM) franchises are high-profile symbolic actions, instead of enacting real programs or policies. Like Jackson's campaigns or Farrakhan in the afterglow of the Million Man March, Sharpton will become a nationally known entity, the putative "president" of black America, the titular head of a purported progressive insurgency—or crash and burn.

Sharpton has long harbored ambitions to be the next HNIC. His recent association with Michael Jackson and the now-forgotten National Summit for Fairness in the Recording Industry held a few summers ago was a means toward a related and specific end: money, media, and prestige. The summit came about as Jackson was in the middle of negotiating his contract with Sony Music. Jackson owed Sony money and may have been trying to sever relations without paying it back and without losing his interest in the 251-song Beatles catalogue, which he owns jointly with Sony. The summit was supposedly held to prod the music industry on behalf of black recording artists, but some suspected that Jackson used it as a means to put pressure on Sony by attracting the public's racially sensitive eye.

A few years earlier Jackson approached Sharpton before a Democratic Party fundraiser at the Apollo and spoke to him about doing something about the music industry; the two of them have known each other since the 1980s. The fundraiser, which raised $2.7 million for the Democratic Party, marked another chapter in the long Jackson-Sharpton relationship. Both men had something the other needed. For Jackson, it was Sharpton's talent at making people squirm when he throws a spotlight on them. For Sharpton, it was the green milk needed to nurse a modern political campaign, media exposure, and legitimacy.

Yet that July 2002 "summit" fizzled in the summer's heat when Jackson called then–Sony head Tommy Mottola a "racist" and rode up Madison Avenue on a double-decker bus holding aloft a caricature that depicted Mottola as a devil. As Jackson made his charges, Sharpton was silent. The following day, however, after being inundated with calls from blacks in the recording industry who took issue with Jackson's antics, Sharpton started moonwalking away from the singer and dancer.

When asked whether he plans to look into Jackson's accusation that Mottola called a Sony artist a "fat, black nigger," Sharpton has said he would be "actively investigating the charge." Needless to say, that investigation, along with the summit's concerns regarding "financial justice" for all black musicians, has since faded with the help of Jackson's idiosyncrasies. The recent re-emergence of alleged child-molestation charges and other curious details concerning Jackson's personal life have only served to further sandbag the original mission of the summit. In essence, however, he performs the necessary sideshow phenomenon of being the Number One freak in America's society of the spectacle.

While the July summit could have been a watershed event, re-establishing a new and fairer relationship between black artists and the recording industry, it also had the earmarkings of a possible post–civil rights shakedown, the kind of politics based mostly on a desire for, in Richard Nixon's words, "a piece of the action."

Usually when a summit or protest march is called and the masses show up, a "leader" feels that his following has achieved a critical mass. He can then represent them before the powers that be (meaning whites, since they are only ones in this country with real power). Said leader can then also negotiate on behalf of another party: himself. Anyone remotely aware of the Rev. Jesse Jackson's recent history might have seen the faintest outlines of such a play in Sharpton's music industry initiative.

It was a convergence of personal agenda, self-interest, and ambition. It was African American power politics masking itself as intervention to end the "economic servitude" of a class of rich musicians at the expense of those less rich. Though Sharpton has claimed that he's following in Jackson's footsteps, he also has in mind another itinerary. As noted by columnist Stanley Crouch:

> Sharpton almost assuredly wants the respect necessary to broker big deals and bring money into the base of his followers, the National Action Network, or to

those who support him locally and nationally. In other words, he wants everything that Jesse Jackson has. If he can master what some call the diversity hustle, he might make it into the boardrooms from which much big dough flows.[9]

It also shows how black music, whether pop or hip-hop, has increasingly been seen as a realm to launch or jump-start would-be political movements. Russell Simmons's alignment with Ben Chavis Muhammad, former head of the NAACP and recently of the "Million Man March" franchise, in establishing the Hip-Hop Summit Action Network (HSAN) is another case in point. As many noted, Simmons's recent threat to protest Pepsi for dissing Ludacris smacked of a Jackson-style shakedown; boycotts and summits are the symbolic tools of the trade for HNICs.

"With [the] hip-hop summits, [Simmons] proved he could deliver a constituency," observed Mark Anthony Neal, author of *What the Music Said* and *Soul Babies*. According to Neal, Simmons now has to prove that this constituency can have an impact on issues and in voting.

To varying degrees, Sharpton, Simmons, and Conrad Muhammad have all crossed swords over who will be the voice of the hip-hop disenfranchised—and who will be the king-maker in New York City Democratic politics. A few years ago, Conrad Muhammad was angry that Sharpton was stealing his thunder. Muhammad was annoyed that Sharpton had usurped his idea for a hip-hop summit attacking rap music's violent and sexually explicit lyrics. Sharpton, who admitted that he didn't know much about hip-hop, has sought street credibility by associating himself with hip-hop artists, most notably by appearing on the cover of the February 2001 issue of *The Source*.

In Neal's view, Sharpton has matured politically in the past ten years. Most importantly, he's "even known by young black folks who don't follow politics."

Black politicos like Sharpton, Simmons, and Minister Conrad Muhammad (founder of Conscious Hip Hop Activism Necessary for Global Empowerment, or CHHANGE) understand that hip-hop culture, as well as being a marketing tool for products, is also the base of an up-and-coming, if yet to be realized, political constituency. (See Simmons's Phat Farm and slavery reparation ads.) The main way to get to that constituency is through music, by linking up the culture industry with politics. In other words, young black consumers (and white ones) are more than just a marketing demographic— they're also a political one. Yet despite Sharpton making a play for the black hip-hop crowd it is whites who are the driving force behind the music as consumers and potential voters, but Sharpton never appeared to go after them the way former Governor Howard Dean of Vermont cultivated his followers, namely through the Internet.

As a former Jackson PR man was reported saying in the *Village Voice*: "Dean was very smart to use the Internet. Ironically, the person who needed the Internet the most was Sharpton. He has less money, less staff, and less sophistication among the people working for him."

The question remains, however: Can Sharpton's candidacy improve the lives of blacks and others by bringing certain issues to the table? There are currently more than 9,000 black elected officials across the nation, and while their election to public office is a testament to the political franchise won by blacks, there is a widespread feeling of disenchantment among black voters about the efficacy of their votes in the American political system, especially in regard to their relationship to the Democratic Party.

As the 1960s black freedom movement moved "from protest to politics," as Bayard Rustin wrote, community and protest leaders became incorporated into the routines of the country's political system. By the 1970s, some of these leaders became, in effect, a national black political directorate, with power centered in the Congressional Black Caucus. Meanwhile, black America retired itself from the kind of political action that disrupted business as usual. Political energy was channeled into voting, the only legitimate form of redress of grievance. Yet despite continuing black discontent, there is still no existing independent black organization comparable to the conservative's Moral Majority or Christian Coalition that can make either the Democrats or Republicans pay attention to black concerns.

In fact Adolph Reed, a New School University professor of political science and a Labor Party organizer, has argued that incumbent black officials have had an incentive not to organize. "It's not in their interest to mobilize new voters or mobilize any dynamic force [in] black politics. Like with the leadership of the civil rights groups, part of their legitimacy historically has been that they can function as alternatives to chaotic or disruptive protest politics."

Part of the current problem, says Reed, is that the class of black political officials who were elected during the 1970s could "reliably get incremental programmatic benefits for their constituents." But what was true under the Nixon, Ford, and Carter administrations no longer holds. In the 1980s, Ronald Reagan and the Republican risorgimento brought an implacable hostility to civil rights concerns, and neither black America nor its leaders were ready for the new regime of race relations, a somewhat less-violent version of Reconstruction politics. Nor were they willing to mobilize as before in response to it. "[Black leaders] haven't been able to respond since then," he added. "They haven't been able to get much in the way of payoffs."

Consequently, since the 1980s, black politics has been faced with a conundrum: it has a leadership class that has institutional means but is unwilling to *risk* to them in order to mobilize its constituents. Freelance racial spokespersons—Jackson, Farrakhan, Sharpton—have sensed this political timidity, but have basically used symbolic mobilization to mask a personalized racial-brokerage politics that has no interest in effective, programmatic politics. Instead, practitioners are merely provided "a seat at the table." Put another way, unaccountable power for the Head Negro in Charge is masked as representing the "interests" of "the black community."

Established black officials are further delegitimized by the need to respond to such forms of politicking as endorsing Jackson's 1988 campaign or by attending the Million Man March. Blacks, in turn, make fewer demands on their leaders and themselves to effect changes within the political system. Everyone settles for the occasional succor of symbolic action.

Within this framework, Sharpton's presidential run has conservative implications.

"It's a way that white politicians and media analysts are accustomed to dealing with black people's interests in politics," says Reed. "That may be more significant and insidious than whatever residue that role has of its own for black people. Sharpton has always been a creature of the mainstream media." Not to say that isn't a virtue. If and when the pooh-bahs in the Democratic Party get their act together and establish a media apparatus, a counterweight to the conservative network of radio and talk shows, Sharpton would be a natural on radio. After all, he is a mouth o'mighty.

As Sharpton said earlier, he wins even when he loses. The long-term outcome, however, will be that when he "wins," effective black politics becomes even more irrelevant than ever before. His idea of "qualification," however, is based on the notion that by dint of him being a "civil rights leader" that he would also be the only black in the Democratic primaries, and that race should suffice to garner votes.

"Without me in the race, it will be part of the exclusive club picture again."[10] However, that claim fell away when former Senator Carol Moseley Braun joined the pack.

Sharpton has run for office three times in the Empire State of New York; twice for a senate seat and once as a mayoral candidate, offices he could not have won. Despite his movement toward conventional Democratic politics, his checkered history revolving around a host of issues and causes over the past fifteen years (e.g., Tawana Brawley; informant for the

FBI; boycotting a Harlem store that led to a mass killing; the Michael Jackson/Sony imbroglio) has prevented him from being taken seriously. To a certain degree, Sharpton is a media creation; a man who would not normally be viewed as a civil rights leader if it were not for the media's need for "good copy."

That he has been "good copy" for the media cements his and movement politics' symbiotic relationship with it. Sharpton is more a celebrity than a "political leader," and his notoriety as such allows him to make a bid to become the next putative leader of black America, the next HNIC. This bid is made possible because black politics is now programmatically and structurally weak, without real accountability from blacks. Increasingly, the certification of black leaders, especially those who are charismatic, takes place through the media, especially television. As Todd Gitlin's *The Whole World is Watching* reminds us:

> From the media point of view, news consists of events which can be recognized and interpreted as drama; and for the most part, news is made by individuals who are certifiably newsworthy. Once an individual has been certified as newsworthy, he or she has been empowered, within limits, to make news.[11]

That has been Sharpton's political project: *making news*, not policies that actually improve the lives of those he claims to speak for. Since the 1960s, movement politics has been increasingly fixated on using the media as a means of organizing—

stating goals and positions, recruitment, media coverage to spotlight issues and grievances, while ignoring the building of consensus, processes, and accountability. "Protest" leaders like Sharpton, seen as "deviant" by American mainstream values, become newsworthy by the very fact that they are "unrepresentative of the values, opinions, passions and practices of the larger society."[12] And that legitimates them in the eyes of others, especially disaffected blacks unserved by their elected officials.

As evidenced by his record above, Sharpton has made *news*. He has legitimated himself as a celebrity *posing* as a political leader, the kind of political leader who has never run for an office he could reasonably win, as in the case of his mentor Jesse Jackson. Instead, he has "pyramided" his celebrity status, "investing media recognition to accumulate more of the same" and turning his "celebrity role to political advantage,"[13] once again like his mentor.

Other than engaging in the pornography of grief by accompanying the relatives of those who have been abused by racist thugs or the NYPD, he has not accomplished anything significant regarding political or social change in the lives of African Americans in the city of New York.

One might conclude that the offices that he could have won—city council, state legislator, or US representative—could have given him the kind of political seasoning, credibility, and track record that would have allowed him to stand for subsequent higher offices. Such offices could have led to the production and implementation of legislation that might improve citizens' lives or enhance their life chances.

But Sharpton, like Jackson, is not really interested in the nuts-and-bolts of representation, i.e., constituent service and problem-solving, but instead in the run for political office's symbolic function: being *the* leader and *articulating* the will of the people. However, in black political culture, based on the charismatic and black church traditions, this effectively means *rhetoric* as *action* in place of action. Sharpton, as it once was said of his former political mentor, isn't really interested in running for political office, he is more invested in "running his mouth."[14] However, given that most blacks are Democrats, the kind of racial-brokerage politics practiced by Jackson and Sharpton allows them to garner black votes as *the* black candidate while not being held responsible for deals they make in the name of the "black community."

This is not to say that Sharpton doesn't have standing with some blacks. And he certainly inherited some after the somnolent administration of New York City's first black mayor, David N. Dinkins, who represented the city's established black leadership's ineffectiveness to an embarrassing degree of perfection. The rise and fall of the Dinkins administration confirmed Martin Kilson's view that New York black politics has been one of weakness and factional division,[15] producing a space for Al Sharpton. Sharpton, on the other hand, has been one of the very few vocal critics of police misconduct in New York City's black and Latino neighborhoods, as in the Abner Louima police-torture case. His marshalling a protest action in response to the shooting of Ghanaian immigrant Amadou Diallo—killed by nineteen bullets in a barrage of forty-one shots by four NYPD police officers in the Bronx—proved this.

Yet it was also this protest and its attendant media coverage at the New York Police Department headquarters that allowed the accused officers' lawyers to obtain a change of venue and take the case out of the city's jurisdiction where the officers where found not guilty before an upstate jury. Like a general who fights today's war with yesterday's tactics and strategies, Sharpton only knows how to do one or two things: protest and symbolic posturing. He is the flip side of the established black leader who neglects direct action as a political tactic along with other considerations.

Sharpton, like Jackson and Farrakhan, is the product of a political subculture that does not hold its representatives accountable, either as insiders or outsiders. As noted by Jerry G. Watts, who was speaking of Amiri Baraka, but could have had the likes of Sharpton, Jackson, and Farrakhan (who we turn to in the next chapter) also in mind:

> Unfortunately, black Americans seem to be too tolerant of irresponsible and unrepresentative political leaders, white and black. It is therefore not surprising that one of the dominant forms of black political leadership is autocracy. In many instances, the very concentration of power in the hands of a few individuals creates charisma around them that gives some blacks a vicarious sense of empowerment. Charismatic leadership, however, is inherently antidemocratic, and is usually incapable of creating authentic mass empowerment.[16]

CHAPTER TWO

FOLLOW THE LEADERS?
THE DEATH OF EFFECTIVE BLACK POLITICS

Louis Farrakhan's self-coronation as the putative HNIC of black America on October 16, 1995, at the "Million Man March" (MMM) was the logical outcome of a long train of social and political events through the course of post–civil rights, post–segregationist America. Since the 1970s, African Americans have been prepared for such an event by the "invented tradition" of Kwanzaa and the pseudo-discipline of Afrocentrism. Both, the first developed by Ron Karenga and the latter fathered by Molefi Kete Asante, have helped to make the rise of Farrakhan possible by creating a culture of "black orthodoxy" or a "cultural politics" through the subtle dismantling of critical thought and the embracing of conspiracy theories. Kwanzaa was invented and has neither a real nor an organic relationship with Africa or with African culture.[1] Yet Kwanzaa is unquestionably accepted and celebrated by many blacks as a social fact from the Motherland. Likewise, Afrocentrism, which had the potential to be a rigorous intellectual discipline that could provide answers to the African past, is a window into a race fantasy in which every black has a noble warrior king as an ancestor. In this culture of orthodoxy any negative action against the black community can be viewed through the prism of blackness or nonblackness. Symbolic political issues like "black reparations" are easier to address than defective public schools. That Russell Simmons can market both "hip-hop" footwear and black reparations in an advertising campaign is further proof of the decline of black political culture and the general hollowing out of African American culture in late capitalism. Worse yet, that Clarence Thomas acceded to the Supreme Court after Thurgood Marshall and that the vast majority of blacks supported him due to "blackness" or "black solidarity" underscores how such black orthodoxy has left African Americans unable to understand who is acting in or against their interests.

Farrakhan's credentials are that he, unlike most of the established black political class, is not part of the dominant political structure, meaning subordinate to the white overclass. Politically, however, Farrakhan's day in the sun was made possible by the black political elite's increasing irrelevance. His rise as a black spokesman signaled the demise of the civil rights establishment and the *deauthorization* of black leaders, political and intellectual. The fact that Farrakhan called for a march and arguably a million or so men answered underscores the political circumstances of African American political leadership. They—the established politicians and academic intellectuals—did not make the call to mass black voices to protest the Republican Right's authoritarian populism or to strategize an agenda against the GOP's "Contract with America." And there is a philosophical meeting of the minds between Farrakhan and some Republicans, noted Robert Evans. In his *New York Post* column he wrote about "How Farrakhan could energize the Republicans," a few years after the march. What made Farrakhan attractive was his "stress on self-help and moral values," which "evoked the longest sustained applause" before a white audience of business executives and supply-siders that Farrakhan addressed in Boca Raton.[2] Small wonder that Farrakhan is favored by some black conservatives as well as their white colleagues. (Given black America's love affair with symbolic politics, one should not be surprised to see a MMM 10th Anniversary Edition of some sort.)

However, more important than the leader of the Nation of Islam proclaiming himself a big-ticket leader was the political fact that for the first time in the postemancipation political history of African Americans, a gathering of black men came together to literally protest *themselves*, as one savvy commentator noted.[3] The subtext of that keen observation was that black politics, like all politics, was no longer a means to an end—the end being to share the material and cultural benefits of American society, with blacks as social equals to their white compatriots—but had morphed into a politics of mere symbolism.

The Nation of Islam leader essentially saw his leadership role as a performance; he was the "premier showman who actually performed leadership."[4] Farrakhan, in the post–civil rights era, was able to do something that established black leaders could not, namely draw large numbers of blacks. The "Million Man March" was the logical culmination of what he had been doing for years. Arguably, by 1995, Farrakhan was the most influential black leader in America, yet he squandered whatever political capital he had accumulated by embarking on a world tour for several months, neglecting the agenda he had offered at the march. Farrakhan, like most of today's black leadership, was better at performing as a leader than actually being one.

Needless to say, the minister of the NOI did *not* hold himself accountable to contributing to the atmosphere that led to the assassination of his mentor, Malcolm X, on that "Day of Atonement." Instead, black America was given insight into white control over the black nation via the myth of Willie Lynch, an alleged white West Indies slavemaster who gave colonial Virginians a discourse, in the early eighteenth century, on how to control slaves. Unfortunately, it is far easier for many to believe in that mythological slavemaster than to take the time to read Eugene Genovese's *Roll, Jordan, Roll: The World the Slaves Made*. And that is exactly the point. Within black political culture, we have witnessed the rise of self-appointed pseudo-leaders who are not accountable for either what they do or say, who trade in myths, fantasies, and rhetoric. Moreover, those who are duly elected— mayors, council people, congressional representatives, etc.— have become increasingly incorporated into the state's apparatus of control and management, and are thus more accountable to those powers than to those from whom they derive their legitimacy, i.e., black voters.

One thing has to be understood. Neither black politics nor black political culture happens in a vacuum. Black politics, like African American culture, is a subculture of American society, yet it has its own logic and history. (After all, who else could have come up with hip-hop, based on rhythmic word-play, scratching James Brown records, spinning on one's head, and becoming a billion-dollar-plus music genre?) However, the dominant political culture cannot be understood without accepting how the black presence has shaped it, just as black politics has to be understood within the context of the broad trajectory of American history, politics, and culture. One of the specifics of African American political culture, namely the significance of the preacher as a political leader, has engendered, if you will, an "Afrocentric" type of charismatic politics with characteristic strengths and weaknesses. Black politics also has to be viewed as having transformed itself in response to the dominant society in at least eight distinct sociopolitical regimes throughout American history:

Black Slavery, Black Freedom, and White Supremacy, 1619–1865

Emancipation, Reconstruction, and Nullification, 1866–1883

The Nadir: Terror, Lynching, and the Reimposition of White Supremacy, 1884–1914

The Struggle for Black Leadership, 1915–1944

The Struggle for Civil Rights or Racial Integration, 1945–1965

The Rise and Fall of Black Power, 1966–1976

The Golden Age of Integration, 1970–1980

The Disappearance of Black Leadership and the Emergence of Symbolic Politics, 1980–present

The Million Man March, actually a rally, represented a shift *away* from results-oriented politics that had been geared toward solving problems like discrimination and racism, or bettering the life chances of blacks through education, voter registration, etc. For the past hundred years black politics had geared itself toward ending de jure and de facto segregation, and challenging white supremacy in its overt and subtle manifestations. Black politics became one of many post-WWII social movements that sought to rectify the second-class status of African Americans. The Montgomery Bus Boycott of 1955 was the mother of all social movements in that it spawned the civil rights movement and other social movements including those of students, Hispanics, women, gays, the disabled, antiwar, Black Power and others during the '60s and '70s. (Even those whites with white-supremacist beliefs seek to model their "movement" after the black freedom struggle.) And that aspect of the black freedom movement was part of a longer process initiated by the 1905 Niagara Movement and the National Association for the Advancement of Colored People (NAACP) in 1909, which encompassed three distinct phases: lobbying, litigation, and protest.[5]

Sensing a vacuum in black political leadership from Jackson's last campaign in 1988, and seeing that nothing happened in regard to effective African American policies—voter mobilization, policy agenda, etc.—from then up to 1995, Farrakhan was able to step into the breach. He learned his lesson well and understood the cardinal rule of all black politicians, elected and nonelected: Neither the black public nor the black electorate will hold you accountable. This lesson has also been learned by the "shadow" Jesse, the Rev. Al Sharpton. What has Farrakhan done with his HNICship since that day in Washington? He has presided over a series of symbolic franchises: the Million Youth March, the Million Women March, etc.

In other words, he has done nothing—and once again, that is the point. Black politics has effectively been demobilized. The rise of the new-jack symbolic politics has been aided and abetted by the political capitulation of the black Democratic political establishment and civil rights movement that has long turned into an *industry* based on affirmative action and minority set-asides for the new black middle class. Farrakhan is merely symptomatic of a political culture that has gone from protest politics to institutional incorporation and has subsisted off of symbolic politics in the aftermath of the civil rights era for about thirty years.

In and of itself, the black freedom movement's political incorporation was not necessarily a bad move or an unfortunate transformation. One can view it as the natural progression of a social movement. All social movements either: a) proclaim victory and place down their ideological "pitchforks"; b) exhaust themselves; c) are repressed; d) cannibalize themselves with factionalism and become marginal; or e) incorporate or institutionalize themselves into the larger political framework. Such incorporation, however, has to be judged on whether it has been effective in terms of the original agenda. The political incorporation of the black freedom movement, while achieving some aims, has not been successful in ameliorating the conditions that confront the lower strata of black America. In the long run, black America has been demobilized, rendering the black political establishment irrelevant.

During the civil rights movement there were four leading organizations: the Southern Christian Leadership Conference (SCLC), the National Association for the Advancement of Colored People, the Congress of Racial Equality (CORE), and the Student Nonviolent Coordinating Committee (SNCC). Of the four, the NAACP was the oldest, had the deepest pockets, and was the most mainstream, if not conservative, of all the organizations. Its foremost expertise was litigating the nation's legally codified segregation laws. CORE came into existence during the late 1940s using the method of direct action in desegregating public accommodations and, as such, spawned the direct action techniques of SCLC and the more radical SNCC. SCLC was essentially the brainchild of Martin Luther King Jr. and was born of his experience as the leader of the Montgomery Bus Boycott of 1955. SNCC was an offshoot of SCLC and came into being during the "wildcat" student sit-ins that ran through the South and the rest of the nation during the early 1960s, "godmothered" by the legendary Ella Baker. All four of the organizations engaged in cooperation, coordination, and competition, showcasing the kind of insider/outsider politics that led to the passage of landmark civil rights legislation in the 1960s.

Of those four leading organizations that saw "action" during the civil rights era, only the NACCP would survive in any meaningful way. Yet even the NAACP now retains only a shadow of the significance it once held in the earlier years of the post–civil rights era. King's SCLC practically died with him in Memphis, if not in the mud of the Poor People's Campaign debacle. SCLC and SNCC had eclipsed CORE by using its technique of direct action during the 1960s. SNCC, with its grassroots projects to raise indigenous Deep South black leadership, often saw the "race problem" not as a moral one rooted in the lack of Christian fellowship, allowing segregation and racism, but as one of deep-seated institutional racism. The reign of violence and constant political disenfranchisement that buffeted Southern blacks during the sixties led SNCC activists to question the politics of coalition-building and integration. Out of that frustration came the cry of "Black Power" on Southern roads. SNCC would not survive and transform itself into the 1970s. Black Power would be its lasting legacy in the era of "black liberation."

By 1965, the main goals of the civil rights movement, as articulated by the earlier Niagara Movement and the NAACP— political, civil, and social rights that demanded an end to discrimination in public accommodations, equal enforcement of the law, and quality education—had mostly been won. These rights can be termed bourgeois democratic rights; however, that made them no less important. For African Americans who had been taxed without discrimination and served in the country's wars before and after slavery, they were the universal rights that all free people in a developed modern democracy had come to expect—particularly Southern blacks. As well as winning the right to vote, Southern blacks were no longer subjected to the regime of terror and intimidation that had plagued them since the end of Reconstruction.

However, the battle for freedom was partially won because vast numbers of blacks experienced poverty and/or chronic unemployment in Southern rural counties and Northern urban centers. In the great migration of the First World War and later, millions of blacks journeyed northward for a better life, only to find discrimination and lack of opportunity there. The Civil Rights Act of 1964 and the Voting Rights Act of 1965 laid the foundation, in the eyes of some civil rights leaders, of moving from protest to developing a political coalition that would institutionalize those newly won rights. Also, the political emphasis would take the movement to the next phase: the *economic justice* aspect of civil rights needed to address the situation of blacks in Northern slums.

Bayard Rustin, the civil rights activist and lieutenant of labor leader A. Philip Randolph, had strategized such a move in "From Protest to Politics: The Future of the Civil Rights Movement," which originally appeared in the February 1965 issue of *Commentary* magazine. He foresaw the need for a "progressive coalition" which would be "the *effective* political majority in the United States" (italics in original) in order to confront the economic infrastructural changes that the next phase of the civil rights movement would need to effect. That coalition would be the same one that staged the march on Washington, passed the civil rights acts, and laid the foundation for the 1964 Johnson landslide, he told readers; it would be a coalition of "Negroes, trade unionists, liberals, and religious groups."[6] In other words, the Democratic Party.

King, however, wanted to continue with a massive protest march to articulate the need for the government and society to address economics issues, as in the Poor People's Campaign, but Rustin balked at organizing such a mobilization.[7] The Poor People's Campaign was the last major demonstration of the civil rights era and occurred after King's death, signaling the end of the usefulness that protest instrument without that charismatic but effective leader. King's legacy would be a multifaceted one, being many things to different people. Other than having the courage of his convictions, he did not leave behind an institution or coherent movement that could carry on his work. Now cynical conservatives cite him as their spiritual godfather for "color-blind" rhetoric when arguing against affirmative action while ignoring that King actually argued for such specific programs for blacks.

From the late 1960s and 1970s onward, due to the Voting Rights Act of 1965, African Americans increasingly won local, municipal, state, and federal offices in the United States. The most important of these offices were at the federal level, in the U.S. Congress, since that branch of government formulates public policies and controls taxation and the allocation of resources. The Congressional Black Caucus (CBC) could been seen as the formation of a national black political directorate which represented, at the federal level, the national black community. Ironically this "directorate" was formed as one of the country's most flamboyant black legislators was on his way out of the halls of Congress. Harlem's Representative Adam Clayton Powell lost his seat to Charles Rangel after a long battle with his Congressional colleagues over ethics charges and partially because of self-inflicted wounds. Powell was rebuked and denied his seat as a representative for misappropriation of funds, and while the Supreme Court reversed that decision, his chronic absences and vacations in Bimini gave his Harlem constituents an opportunity to reassess their relationship with him. In 1970, Powell lost his seat to Rangel.

This was also the era, the apogee, of Black Power consciousness, which all strata of black America accepted to varying degrees. To be clear, blacks as individuals and as members of different social classes accepted the general outlines, in a vague consensus of black power and racial solidarity. It was this vagueness that would lead to the "fracturing" of post–civil rights solidarity in the wake of King's death, on account of two competing agendas: the politics of incorporation and the politics of "unity without uniformity" of the black nationalist wing. However, it suffices to say that Black Power consciousness laid the groundwork for a criterion of *black orthodoxy*, in which all issues have to be discussed or acted upon in terms of the concept of "blackness," irrespective of whether blackness has any legitimate answers or responses to certain critical issues facing African Americans.

Given the civil rights movement's institutional incorporation, the integration wing proved more successful than the Black Power contingent, which was largely ignored by blacks (but accepted in regard to some cultural issues), but repressed by agencies of the state, especially by the FBI's COINTELPRO, which spied on King, Malcolm X, and the Nation of Islam, as well as targeting the SNCC, the Black Panthers, and others. However, the success of the other wing's incorporation also exposed the new black political elite's very weakness. Robert C. Smith has argued that while the pro–civil rights consensus in Congress won more than a dozen civil rights or race-specific bills or amendments, "these victories [were] to an extent irrelevant, symbolic as much as substantive insofar as the life chance of blacks in the United States today."[8] Bills like the Humphrey-Hawkins Full Employment Act in 1978, aimed at easing chronic black unemployment, wound up being passed as watered-down symbolic gestures with no real effect. Interestingly, as Smith has noted, the "ghetto constituents" toward whom such bills were aimed were not mobilized:

> This means that the leadership of black America needs to direct its attention more to mobilization of its ghetto constituents and less to building coalitions from the top in Washington. *If* effective government actions are to be taken to deal with the problem of ghetto joblessness and poverty, the black community itself must be mobilized into sustained movement of internal redevelopment and external protest and politics. A movement that would be so powerful in its pressure that the system would have to go beyond its now routine of neglect and symbolism (original italics).[9]

It must also be noted that the most important pieces of civil rights legislation—the Civil Rights and Voting Rights acts of the 1960s—had already been passed. Black leadership—political, economic, and intellectual—had boxed blacks into a corner by becoming overly dependent on one method of ameliorating years of political and economic disenfranchisement through affirmative action and top-down racial management. The black elite has never really been interested in "internal redevelopment," and has often viewed affirmative action programs as means to that end. In doing so, it has made a "tacit" agreement, as argued by Michael Lind, in *The Next American Nation*, not to disrupt the status quo.[10]

In other words, there will be no more leaders like Martin, Malcolm, Rustin, or Randolph, because the new post–civil rights black bourgeoisie has no interest in nurturing such people. Instead, into the breach have stepped Jesse, Louis, and Al with symbolic politics rooted in the charismatic, authoritarian, and rhetorical tradition of America's black political culture.

What black America has witnessed and experienced in the post–civil rights era is the bifurcation of black leadership and the black community, a breaking of the "bonds of solidarity" that were forged in the caldron of slavery and in the post–Civil War years, in Reconstruction, and post-Reconstruction. There is no longer *a* black community but there are black communit*ies*. Black America is riven by class interests and those interests have become pronounced in the aftermath of integration: Namely, those with talent, skills, and education have taken advantage of the openings and opportunities of postsegregationist America. Also, from the 1970s, the US economy began to shift, with a decline in the nation's manufacturing base. This resulted in the loss of low-skilled but well-paid employment in the nation's cities with sizable black populations. A spatial shift also occurred in that manufacturing jobs first moved out of the urban centers and then to the suburbs or rural areas, and then out of the country. With these economic developments came also a shift in family and social mores that once knitted together a communal life for rural and urban black America.

This bifurcation also left the young urban blacks with a questionable heritage of "black orthodoxy," fertile ground for alternative views of reality grounded in the bling-bling hip-hop lifestyle, or the worldviews of Afrocentrism, Kwanzaa, etc. Integration also meant that those with the wherewithal, the middle class, could now move away from black neighborhoods, leaving black enclaves with newly emerging role models: drug dealers and pimps. Young children and teens no longer saw the doctor, the lawyer, the businesswoman, or the radical black activist or militant as providing alternatives to the harsh realities of ghetto life. "Gettin' over" became the predominant ethos, a way of life characterized in *Superfly* and Curtis Mayfield's soundtrack, and in hip-hop music thirty years later with rappers like 50 Cent portraying "the crazy nigga." Films like *The Godfather* showed how another ethnic group (Italians, who later became "white") achieved power, and *Scarface* reaffirmed the same story of illegitimate upward mobility for the crack-cocaine '80s and is now a touchstone for some members of the hip-hop generation.

As the civil rights movement became institutionalized it tactically demobilized itself by no longer energizing a black constituency in the inner cities or in the rural South. It shifted away from direct action: protests, sit-ins, marches, development of parallel institutions, the disruption of business as usual. Granted, it may have been difficult to continue this mass-based form of politics, because social movements tend to exhaust themselves over a period of time. However, movements like the Black Panther Party, while of an oppositional Marxist-Leninist nature, showed that inner city youths could be mobilized. Also, the subsequent rise of hip-hop music also shows that black youth have always been ready to receive the word of engagement if given guidance and groomed for future leadership positions. The rise of hip-hop is testament to the creativity of African American culture, yet it shows how HNICs who appeal to the authoritarian-charismatic tendency in black political culture can easily hijack it.

During both the Reagan and George H.W. Bush administrations, African Americans never held a single march or rally of the size or the significance of the 1963 March on Washington or the MMM during the Clinton years. The Reagan-Bush years were the years of the most dramatic black political retreat. There may have been a memorial march commemorating the historic 1963 march, but it was symbolic and wasn't aimed at countering the draconian policies and anti–civil rights hostility of those two administrations. Moreover, it had no sustained political follow-up. And, despite the legislative "victories" of the CBC, they all tended to be within the narrow framework of civil rights. The CBC spearheaded the repeal of the Byrd Amendment, which permitted the importation of chrome from Rhodesia (now Zimbabwe) in violation of UN sanctions; it also strengthened the Voting Rights Act in 1970, 1972, and in 1985. It made President Reagan back down from supporting tax exemptions to educational institutions that practiced racial discrimination; it helped override Reagan's veto of the Martin Luther King Jr. holiday. The CBC imposed sanctions on South Africa (overriding a Reagan veto), and participated in preventing Robert Bork from obtaining a seat on the Supreme Court.

Once again, taken as a whole, these efforts were symbolic insofar as they did not by and large alter or enhance the life chances of blacks in the United States. To do so would require another sort of work—"internal redevelopment"— by the new black elite, and that new class, over the past thirty years, has been seduced away from that task by its association with America's power elite. Yet during Adam Clayton Powell's tenure as chairman of the House Committee on Education and Labor he managed the passage of legislation that created Medicare, Medicaid, and Head Start, along with an increase in the minimum wage. Powell accomplished this during his short reign as chairman while the CBC has experienced exponential growth but a record of lackluster political results, particularly in bettering life for African Americans. (It should be noted that Powell's chairmanship was not held in high regard by some of his Congressional colleagues.)

The missing component of the civil rights movement was a consideration of *self-generated* black economic development. However, such a thing smacked of mom-and-pop black nationalism of the Nation of Islam sort, circa Elijah Muhammad. Yet not to do so, and to continue to depend on federal assistance policies or to long for the Urban League's often-touted "Urban Marshall Plan" has left blacks exposed and vulnerable. Historically the organization at the forefront of agitating for black inclusion in the American way of life—

the NAACP—has had a policy of *noneconomic liberalism*. This policy was predicated on the naïve notion that African Americans need not develop their own program of economic development in a marketplace society. After all, it was thought that if blacks could actually integrate, they would have free and unfettered access to the country's economic system. The Depression of the 1930s exposed the fallacy of the NAACP's position, though Franklin D. Roosevelt's New Deal saved the organization from having to revamp its priorities.

The NAACP, the premier civil rights organization, has thus never had to consider a comprehensive economic program. What passes for one today is a program centered merely on homeownership and small business development ("Home Ownership and Business Initiative"). It was W.E.B. Du Bois, while still an active member of the NAACP, who pressed for an effective program ("Cooperative Commonwealth"), but he did so after having taken issue, years earlier, with Booker T. Washington's emphasis on economics over politics. Transforming the civil rights movement into institutional politics, without a relatively independent political and economic base, exposed the flaw in Rustin's thinking as a democratic socialist. To this day, a third of black America is trapped within the walls of either unemployment or underemployment, and the new middle class that has come into existence via federally assisted programs like affirmative action may not be able to socially reproduce itself without government assistance.

This does not mean that African Americans should forgo making demands on resources that are their rights as citizens; it means, though, that blacks have been weak in cultivating a menu of various options—protests, affirmative action, coalition politics, self-generated economic activities, etc. To use a military analogy, the United States has various services (army, navy, air force, and marines) and uses them either individually or collectively depending on the mission. The United States has an array of options when it decides to use force. Blacks, however, have tactically and strategically limited themselves to one or two tactics and strategies since the 1960s when they last used insider and outsider politics to press for black freedom.

A large part of the reason why black leadership is seen as irrelevant is its failure to address the question of economic development and its inability to improve black life for those in the lower socioeconomic strata. Black Democrats have acquiesced in policies and served interests that do not help blacks, and their support for Bill Clinton and his perverse reciprocity clearly showed that. The Clinton administration sent more people to jail than either of the previous two Republican administrations: 673,000 were sent to state and federal prisons under Clinton; 343,000 under Bush; 488,000 under Reagan. During Clinton's two terms, *black* incarceration rates rose to 3,620 per 100,000 from around 3,000 per 100,000 people, according to the Justice Policy Institute, an offshoot of the Center on Juvenile and Criminal Justice.[11] These incarceration rates also affect black electoral participation since virtually all states deny the right to vote to ex-felons even after they have finished their sentences.

The national Democratic Party, the party of most black federal, state, and local elected officials, treats the black vote as a dependable booster component: It rockets white candidates into the orbit of elections, yet black concerns are later routinely jettisoned and treated as "special interests." The Democrats, led by the Democratic Leadship Council, desires the electorate of choice, meaning white suburban voters who generally are afforded quality, decent education for their children. However, the GOP, under the present Bush administration, has successfully co-opted the Democrats' position on education. They are considered more trustworthy on that issue than the Democrats.[12]

Or consider President George W. Bush's faith-based initiatives. The irony is that the civil rights movement began as a "faith-based initiative," yet the civil-rights-movement-turned-industry couldn't even strategize a way to get money from the government to support black church programs that have a track record of qualitatively improving individual lives. It took a "compassionate conservative" Texas Republican. The Democrats have such a low regard for their most loyal constituents that they would rather have had Trent Lott remain in the position of Senate majority leader because "That would present them with a high-profile target to mobilize Democratic voters, particularly blacks, over the next two years."[13] Now that the Mississippian has vacated that position, the Democrats may have to devise a new program to ignite their black voting base.

The fact that lower-income blacks would consider the questionable school voucher plan proffered by the GOP shows how utterly bereft that class of African Americans is of effective leadership that would help them solve pressing problems like the education of their children. That one does not find Jesse Jackson, Representative Charles Rangel, the NAACP, the Urban League, or so-called black public intellectuals speaking on such issues speaks volumes about the disappearance of effective black leadership from the lives of ordinary blacks. Essentially, the national black political directorate that came into being during the 1970s has transformed itself into a compradorian class of agents who act as intermediaries between the white overclass and an *imaginary* black community. Its supreme goal, it would seem, is to deliver the black vote without disturbing the concerns of white swing or independent voters.

Yet the Republicans are gaining traction on issues like education with the same cunning that has already been successful for them, namely finding blacks who are willing to spearhead such issues and support them either financially or through a network or infrastructure that promotes their views. In other words, the Republicans have been successful at manufacturing a black counterestablishment to discredit liberal orthodoxy or roll back the gains of the civil rights era.

There is no better example of this than the rise of Shelby Steele, previously an obscure teacher of Afro-American literature at San Jose State University, but now a fellow at the conservative Hoover Institution at Stanford University who specializes in race. What catapulted Steele into the legion of public intellectuals was the publication of *The Contents of Our Character*, which won a National Book Critics Circle Award in 1990. Subsequent to that he appeared on *Nightline* and the *McNeil/Lehrer NewsHour*, and was profiled in the *New York Times* and the *Washington Post*. Steele's book was the beginning of a trend of "racial realist" writing that faults blacks for not living up to mainstream American values and scorns the "social engineering" of the Great Society initiatives of the 1960s. In reality, Steele is similar to a number of new-jack black intellectuals—left, right, and center—who have learned that the dominant society offers far greater rewards for black-bashing than for assisting black America. Interestingly, Steele, previously unknown for any scholarly work in black literature, faults blacks for being racially obsessive while he himself has now made a career of race.[14]

The failure of black politics, however, isn't solely the fault of black elected officials, even though they have been at the helm of the national black political directorate for the past thirty years. As I suggested earlier, the fault also lies with the intelligentsia, meaning black intellectuals, be they conservative or so-called oppositional public intellectuals. Regardless of their ideological positions on certain issues, black intellectuals are members of the new black bourgeoisie that has come into existence during the past thirty years of the postsegregationist regime. Black conservative intellectuals, to a certain degree, are a "manufactured" creation of the white conservative movement. They have been nurtured, if not created, by a white conservative movement and infrastructure via think tanks and foundations. In the view of Walters and Smith:

> Black conservatives in America do not have a mass
> constituency in the Black community or linkage with

institutions indigenous to Black America. Nor have they sought to build such a constituency or such linkages. Rather, *their role is not to lead Black people but to lead White opinion about Black people.*[15] (Italics added.)

And they have spectacularly and successfully done so, as "market intellectuals" along with their left-of-center counterparts. Black conservatives and the GOP often cite polls saying that most blacks are socially conservative. But something else ought to be considered. Is this "conservatism" ideologically based, i.e., "black conservatism" in the sense of a set of fixed ideas and principles aimed at a political end? Or is it traditionalism rooted in past practices and a sense of things handed down from time immemorial, in the sense of conservative blacks? If the latter, it may explain why blacks, though socially conservative, still tend to vote for policies that support their interests, if not their ideological orientation. Also, most voting-age blacks understand the policies of people like Richard Nixon, Ronald Reagan, Barry Goldwater, Jesse Helms, Patrick Buchanan, Rush Limbaugh, William F. Buckley, and others who were and still are opponents of black advancement, and they have made sure that socially conservative blacks have not become black conservatives.

There have been a number of books, reports, and articles over the years that have looked at how conservative think tanks and foundations have influenced the country's social and public policy agenda, and the role of black and other nonwhite intellectuals.[16] As noted in Covington's "Moving a Public Policy Agenda: The Strategic Philanthropy of Conservative

Foundations,"; Stefancic and Delagado's *No Mercy: How Conservative Think Tanks and Foundations Changed America's Social Agenda*, and Blumenthal's *The Rise of a Counter-Establishment: From Conservative Ideology to Political Power*, the modus operandi has been to construct a network or infrastructure and then recruit willing and able black intellectuals or pundits like Thomas Sowell, Shelby Steele, Alan Keyes, Clarence Thomas, Glenn Loury (who has recently jumped ship), Armstrong Williams, and others to attack and undermine programs and issues like affirmative action and welfare, and to criticize the so-called underclass and black behavior, as opposed to white racism or institutional racism. The post–civil rights, liberal integrationist black elite was not ready for the ideological onslaught of the Reagan administration. Reagan himself ignored established black leadership and tried to create his own sort of black establishment by bestowing recognition on like-minded black conservatives.[17]

As stated above, conservatives have been successful in severely wounding, if not totally destroying, the civil rights agenda and the legacy of the New Deal and the Great Society programs. While they have effectively undermined the legitimacy of Aid to Families with Dependent Children (AFDC), they have been less successful with affirmative action given the recent Supreme Court decision in *Grutter v. Bollinger*, which supports affirmative action programs in college selection as a means of promoting diversity. However, the conservatives' overall success has been in setting the terms of debate over public policy. For example, Clinton, a moderate Democrat (or an Eisenhower Republican), used the conservative attack on welfare to boast of "ending welfare as we know it" (read: "doing something about those lazy blacks") and later signed the GOP's Welfare Reform Act of 1996, an election year.

In essence, the conservatives understand the essential goal of propaganda and advertising: It is not necessarily important what one says but *who says it.* A black castigating welfare and the moral depravity of the black underclass cannot be called a racist even if the intent is aimed at a specific sector of society, meaning blacks. Black conservatives function as "pet Negroes" within the conservative movement and the Republican Party, giving cover to whites' racist sentiment masquerading as public policy, and are protected by conservative whites as "courageous individuals" when attacking the liberal consensus on race management. What is also interesting to note is that black conservatives never appear in some of the aforementioned books as *original* thinkers or strategists of conservative thought, policies, or tactics. This lends credence to the charge that black conservatives are only viewed as "vanguard thinkers" if they are in lockstep with their white conservative counterparts. The case of Glenn Loury bears this out.[18] Yet some of their criticisms may have merit if they are considered self-correction mechanisms and not the machinations of the conservative wing of the white overclass. However, a problem is that black political culture has a tendency not to tolerate or foster "loyal opposition" criticism as a means of self-correction on either side of the political spectrum.

Even if black conservatives are suspect, so-called black public intellectuals on the other side of the political spectrum have to share the burden of the established black elite's dismal record of leadership during the past thirty years. The gravy-train years of the 1970s, the golden age of the post–civil rights era, led black Americans into a false sense of security and did not prepare them for the Republican risorgimento of the 1980s. (Interestingly, William Julius Wilson's *The Declining Significance of Race* [1978] was published in this era before the GOP's twelve-year regime.)

Some of the reaction to black progress could have been reasonably foretold by reading some earlier post-emancipation history, and discerning a fundamental social law. Any sustained concerted effort to alleviate the status of African Americans will result in a subsequent period of reaction. This happened during Reconstruction, 1865–1877, and the years of lynching and political disenfranchisement began after 1877. Tomes such as C. Vann Woodward's *The Strange Career of Jim Crow* and his *Reunion and Reaction*, Du Bois's *Black Reconstruction*, and Rayford Logan's *The Betrayal of the Negro*, all written before the civil rights era, outlined the regime of oppression that confronted blacks in the postbellum period of the nineteenth century and well into the twentieth century. The 1980s were no different (albeit without the systematic physical violence directed at blacks by terrorist organizations like the Ku Klux Klan), but blacks either didn't see the retrenchment coming or didn't want to believe what was unfolding before their eyes. Surprisingly, there has been very little critical or historical accounting of the *post*–civil rights era on a par with Taylor Branch's work on the civil rights era in *Parting the Waters*. There is a trove of material on political science, and cultural aspects of black history, but so-called black public intellectuals have not taken up this challenge.

The rise of black studies in the universities and the increased presence of black students has not necessarily meant a concomitant rise in the number of black intellectuals committed to a serious examination of black life nor the problems facing those at the lower end of the economic food chain, or the general political fortunes of the black body politic. And despite the rise of a new black middle class, there has not been an increase in the number of journals concerning public affairs or black culture within a black public sphere. As a matter of fact, the post–civil rights generations, those who came of age during the sixties and after, tend to support consumer-lifestyle publications: beauty, sports, music. After a run of about ten years, *Emerge*, a black version of *Time* or *Newsweek*, so to speak, was cancelled by BET's former owner Robert Johnson, and replaced with *Savoy*, another lifestyle magazine (which recently went bankrupt). Whites, however, on the left, center, and right, have *The Nation*, *The Progressive*, *The American Prospect*, *Atlantic Monthly*, *Harper's*, *Commentary*, *The Weekly Standard*, and *The National Review*: journals of public affairs, politics, and opinion. In other words, the post–civil rights intelligentsia has failed to establish a serious intellectual or cultural apparatus outside of the white mainstream, media outlets that could pose the all-important question, What's going on?

Instead, there is a surfeit of hip-hop or neo-hip-hop magazines: *Vibe*, *4 Front*, *F.E.D.S.*, *The Source*, *XXL*, *King*, *The Next Level*, *Elemental*, *Don Diva*. For lifestyle and hair care, blacks read *Savoy*, *Floss*, *Black Hair*, *Hype Hair*, *Sister 2 Sister*, *Honey*, *Essence*, *Heart & Soul*, and others. *Ebony*, along with its sister publication *Jet*, is the closest to being a general interest publication, but it still tends to focus on how many shoes certain black celebrities have in their closets. *Black Enterprise* is primarily a booster magazine about a vanishingly marginal activity in America, namely black business. *The Crisis*, the house organ of the NAACP, is the closest to being a public affairs journal, but its distribution is probably as limited as its influence. Years ago *The Crisis* was part of a triumvirate that also consisted of the Urban League's *Opportunity* and *The Messenger*. Gone or nearly gone are *The Negro Digest*, *Freedomways*, *The Black World*, and *The Black Scholar*. There is nary a general-interest public-affairs journal despite blacks spending $600–$700 billion as consumers.[20a] Whites have more music and lifestyle magazines than blacks since they are the majority population, but they also have numerous journals and periodicals devoted to news, public affairs, politics, and opinion. While one might consider it noteworthy that blacks do have something to read, it's best to consider Mark Twain's acerbic observation: "The man who doesn't read good books has no advantage over the man who can't read."

Instead, blacks are left with NPR and PBS programs that feature Tavis Smiley in which schmoozing replaces asking hard questions or providing critical insight. Blacks receive heaping doses of afro-kitsch and vacuous "brother, brother" soul-talking. To paraphrase Neil Postman, blacks are amusing themselves to death—but they are taking care of their hair while they do it.

•   •   •

African American politics, particularly those pursued and

articulated by the post–civil rights establishment, especially the likes of Al Sharpton, have been restricted solely to the context of *civil rights*, which has meant petitioning the government for redress of grievances or black recognition. This orientation is crippling. For example, the problems of economic development or job creation need government intervention, something which the movement called for during the early 1960s.

The federal government did step in and intervene with Southern blacks' right to vote, to have equality under the law, and to access the same services that were afforded to whites, one of which was a decent education. Yet both the Kennedy and Johnson administrations had to deal with the resentment of Southern whites and their relationship with the Democratic Party. Forced to deal with the embarrassing display of the US "race problem" before the world while fighting Communism, confronted by nonviolent but persistent direct actions at sit-ins, demonstrations, and freedom rides, the Democratic administrations sent in marshals, the army, and the FBI, and submitted landmark legislation to Congress on public accommodations, voting, and housing. This legislation—principally the Civil Rights Act of 1964 and the Voting Rights Act of 1965— was possible because of the coalition of white liberals, church activists, labor, blacks, and others who supported Johnson in the 1964 election.

As Rustin had articulated earlier, this was the sort of coalition that would be needed to move to the next phase, namely "economic justice." Blacks would have the vote but nothing to vote for if they had neither jobs nor education. One of the goals of the 1963 March on Washington for Jobs and Freedom was to motivate the government toward job creation as well as the enforcement of basic civic and democratic freedoms for blacks. Even with the passage of the new civil rights laws, and with their necessary enforcement in litigation, a significant segment of blacks still faced chronic unemployment or underemployment, and both situations were doubly exacerbated in the Northern slums. This was a mass problem that would require the concentrated efforts of a government.

The threat of a good example does work; one should recall that the 1963 march was based on the threat of another mobilization: A. Philip Randolph's call for a march on Washington during the Second World War. In the early 1940s, the country's war industries remained segregated. President Franklin Roosevelt issued an executive order that established the Fair Employment Practices Commission (FEPC), which ensured that blacks were given wartime defense employment. Likewise, during the Cold War, the threat of a new march on Washington, in the aftermath of the SCLC's triumph in Birmingham, was the movement's bid to make the Kennedy administration contend with a national problem that was often treated merely as a local concern before the international community.

With the passages of the 1964–65 civil rights acts and the explosively hot summers of black discontent, the movement began articulating a new agenda: "economic justice." Like political justice—blacks obtaining a free and unfettered franchise, and equal access to public accommodations—economic justice meant that a systematic and systemic approach would be needed to address the "economic subordination of the

American Negro." Not only that, but the problem of job creation for all Americans needed to be addressed as well as "fundamental economic inequality along racial lines." Rustin and two of his assistants, Norman Hill and Tom Khan, drafted a memo that detailed ideas for a "two-day mass descent" on the legislative and executive branches in Washington. This was to be a peaceful but purposeful assembly of citizens, allied with the church and labor, armed with special legislation presented on the first day, and a procession down Pennsylvania Avenue culminating in a rally at the Lincoln Memorial on the second day.[20]

When President Kennedy kept dodging a meeting with King to avoid the civil rights leader's call for a new "Emancipation Proclamation" against segregation, King decided to ally himself with Randolph, who, as a social-democratic labor leader, sought to prod the government and society into "economic justice." Medicare, Medicaid, Head Start, the war on poverty, the Great Society, and its Model Cities program—all bear the markings and philosophy of an activist government in the then-recent tradition of FDR's New Deal.

Yet civil rights as economic justice, along with the burgeoning US presence in South Vietnam, would divert the civil rights leadership from considering the role of internal redevelopment—self-generated economic activity by blacks in a marketplace economy. Randolph's orientation was basically that of a homegrown labor socialist tradition, and organizations like the NACCP advocated a noneconomic liberalism by default, which meant they had no economic program at all. The only organization that had anything near to an economic agenda was Elijah Muhammad's Nation of Islam. Granted, it was bean-pie capitalism, but Muhammad had the foundation of an economic model that mirrored that of Main Street Republicanism (thrift, sobriety, industriousness)— except for the NOI's whites-as-devils philosophy.

The 1963 March on Washington was a combination of symbolic and effective mass mobilization under middle-class leadership of the old Negro school: men like Randolph, the NAACP's Roy Wilkins, and Whitney Young of the Urban League, and also King. These were racial spokesmen, the last generation of "race men." And this class of leaders, along with the everyday people of the Southern masses, would tear down the walls of the most egregious forms of segregation. Yet the mass mobilization of that period, strangely enough, left no permanent *independent* mass-organization down South or in any other part of the country. Instead, the increasing interest in black voting, as opposed to direct-action confrontations over segregation, allowed the Democratic Party to weather Southern whites' defection to the Republicans. By 1972, close to a thousand blacks had won elective office in the South. By the 1976 presidential election, 3.5 million African Americans had been added to voter rolls down South, and Jimmy Carter won the White House because of the black vote. In other words: "The reorganization of the Southern wing of the Democratic Party had succeeded. In virtually no time at all the [civil rights] movement had been incorporated into the electoral system, its leaders running for office throughout the South . . ."[21]

Unlike today's symbolic marches and summits, the 1963

March on Washington had a positive impact in enhancing the life chances of then-Negroes with the passages of major civil rights legislation and programs like Head Start and Medicaid, but more was needed. By 1965, though, the movement was shifting from protest and into symbolic politics—the leaders had failed to understand that the movement's success still depended on direct-action tactics, both for "economic justice" and electoral politics. Furthermore, because it didn't have an independent political apparatus, the black vote became a dependable adjunct to the Democratic Party. Unlike the civil rights movement, the conservative movement, which learned from the civil rights movement and the New Left, established independent organizations—the Moral Majority and the Christian Coalition—*and* burrowed into the GOP. Granted, whites, as liberals or as conservatives, have more resources than blacks, but the point is that conservatives have been more successful than the civil rights movement because they have independent political organizations and a propaganda network that allows them to effectively compete. In the political arena, conservatives understand the value of their vote. Given how American politics operates, it is questionable whether African Americans truly understand the value of their vote, its strength and weakness. While they have been chided for "dependency" (i.e., on "government handouts"), the true dependency occurred with the black vote being enfolded into the Democratic Party without true reciprocity. However, an even greater dependency is the Democratic Party's need for the black vote without genuine reciprocity.

Politics in America, however, not only depends on understanding the necessity of the vote but also knowing its limitations. While voting is important, it has a limited effect on political decisions about income, housing, occupation, and the life chances of voters, especially black voters. These are concerns outside the political spectrum, in the economic sphere, in which blacks are vulnerable, and to which black leadership has traditionally not given much thought except in the context of civil rights or redistributive tax politics. Historically speaking both Booker T. Washington and Du Bois were right; the vote doesn't mean much if you're hungry (Washington), but, when you have the right to eat and work, you need the vote to protect your right to continue to do so (Du Bois). Black leadership's historical failure has been its inability to synthesize the two positions of Washington and Du Bois into a workable program of engaging the present and planning for the future. Black intellectuals have never really synthesized the previous ideas and programs of others into workable political or economic concepts. To date, the best-known black-oriented think tank, the Joint Center for Political and Economic Studies, produces neutered analyses of black voting patterns and political profiles of African American issues, but doesn't develop ideas or programs, unlike the conservative Heritage Foundation, AEI, or the Manhattan Institute. Blacks are intellectually outnumbered and outgunned in policy debates and are thus left using tactics, or more likely the mere rhetoric, of moral suasion from public pseudo-intellectuals.

Without considering internal redevelopment, especially

the role of black business and entrepreneurship, the civil rights leadership from the sixties and seventies narrowed any consideration of economics to the passing of legislation like the Humphrey-Hawkins Full Employment Act, or continued support for affirmative action programs. Economic development was either thought to be an extension of civil rights—meaning couched in terms of the extension or advancement of these rights via court adjudication—or scorned as the "self-help" dribble of the theoretically impaired by the left-of-center intellectuals. Conservatives, black and white, would later use the mantra of "self-help" as a social value behavior dart aimed at welfare and affirmative action policies.

Yet the post–civil rights leadership of the 1970s never articulated a full-throated economic agenda beyond periodic calls for an urban Marshall Plan or advocating that the poor have easier access to relief (welfare). The Black Panther Party's "Ten Point Program" was the closest thing to it, but it ceased to be operational as a "demand by the people" by Jimmy Carter's election in 1976. Nixon toyed with promoting "black capitalism," but that disappeared along with the concern over Black Power by the mid-seventies. In denial, the black leadership has refused to accept that economic justice must be dealt with as an internal project within black America.

W. E. B. Du Bois once proposed that blacks engage in strategic self-segregation in order to tackle certain problems that the dominant society would not voluntarily address in the black community, and then integrate into the majority society from a position of strength. He argued in *Dusk of Dawn* that a black economy was not yet complete but was nonetheless critical to the development of black communities:

> It is quite possible that it [a black economy] could never cover more than the smaller part of the economic activities of Negroes. Nevertheless, it is also possible that this smaller part could be so important and wield so much power that its influence upon the total economy of Negroes and the total industrial organization of the United States would be decisive for the great ends toward which the Negro moves.[22]

The task was ignored, and continues to be in the postsegregationist climate.

While Randolph, Rustin, King, and others were correct in assessing that the next phase of the civil rights struggle had to be economic, the leadership naïvely believed that this could be done by the same old political coalition of liberals, churches, labor, and the federal government. This would mean that blacks had no fallback position during the 1970s and later when the US economy began to restructure and the post–civil rights retrenchment began. With the economic pie getting smaller, whites easily began to feel that they had "done enough" for blacks.

The struggles of the sixties were led by a coalition that used a series of tactics and strategies to confront the nation's apartheid regime, yet black politics disarmed itself when the leadership stopped considering protest or other forms of direct action as a complement to its strategy of political inclusion and electoral politics. Along with that, it never developed, as Harold Cruse argued, a "new institutionalism" that could "intelligently blend privately-owned, collectively-owned, cooperatively-owned, as well as state-sponsored economic organizations."[23] Today's cry for "reparations" not only harks back to the lost cause of "forty acres and a mule" but also the botched "economic justice" agenda of the civil rights era. Yet some blacks believe that there is a pot of gold that the United States government will turn over to them. However, they are only acting out a defective political history that has been bequeathed to them. That earlier generation of blacks, as Cruse noted, believed "it could seek civil rights without seeking group political power, and then demand economic equality in the integrated world without having striven to create any kind of ethnic economic base in the black world."[24]

While some have cited welfare dependency as a cause of continuing black poverty, another argument can be made that blacks' relationship with the Democratic Party is one of disabling dependence. Also, there is no longer a King, a Malcolm X, or a Randolph to point the way to the promised land or map out a strategy that would challenge the powers that be, holding their feet to the fire. The only organization that could fulfill that function is the NAACP, and it is arguably a subsidiary of the Democratic Party.

So, today's generation demands "reparations" without an effective political apparatus, because the previous generation dissolved it when it thought it could win "economic justice" for blacks on the cheap. That generation's greatest failure was its inability to realize that the triumph of the civil rights movement was based on a unique set of historical circumstances—black self-determination, unique individuals as well as ordinary people, coalition politics, domestic and international Cold War politics—that cannot be repeated. Drunk on nostalgia, it has the tendency to repeat the tactics of the past, thinking that the strategies of yesterday can be dragged into the future with the same effect.

Inheriting these assumptions and the thin institutional heritage of the civil rights era, the post–civil rights leadership has been politically coopted and reduced to functional irrelevance, effectively consolidating black America's political demobilization. Even more tragic was the post–civil rights leadership's failure to take advantage of the unique set of circumstances that was handed to it after the civil rights movement.

It is one of the greatest stories *never* told.

The Roots of Symbolic Politics, 1965–1975: The Rise and Fall of Black Power Nationalism

The Fragmenting of the Civil Rights Movement: Black Power

On June 16, 1966, in Greenwood, Mississippi, along the route of a previously attempted march, Stokely Carmichael articulated a new but controversial direction for the black freedom movement in two words: Black Power. The SCLC's Martin Luther King Jr., (who had been awarded the Nobel Peace Prize in 1964), Carmichael (SNCC's new chairman), and other black marchers were completing James Meredith's "march against fear." Meredith, who had integrated the University of Mississippi, had begun a pilgrimage from Memphis into Mississippi on June 5 to demonstrate against the "all-pervasive and overriding fear that dominates the day-to-day life of the Negro in the United States, especially in the South and particularly in Mississippi."[1] However, Meredith was shot and wounded on the second day of his trek, and a call went out to other civil rights leaders to complete the march.

The march began again on June 7, where Meredith had left off, on US 51, but SNCC deftly excluded the NAACP and the Urban League from participation. Carmichael took issue with the NAACP's Roy Wilkins and Whitney Young of the Urban League for wanting to center the march on President Johnson's latest civil rights bill; Carmichael wanted to focus on ending blacks' fear of whites and morally indicting the President. Wilkins and Young balked at SNCC's "manifesto" that called upon the president to make good on previous promises. Needless to say, the two organizations refused to endorse the march. King, however, remained oddly silent; perhaps he wanted to hold the middle ground, perserving what was left of the movement's unity.[2]

The civil rights movement was at a crossroads, a victim both of its own success and of changing times. Since 1955, when King and fellow black citizens of Montgomery, Alabama, boycotted that city's segregated bus line, King had defined the civil rights era for a decade by stressing nonviolence in the African American struggle against second-class citizenship and white supremacy. The movement was primarily four operational groups: SNCC, the NAACP, CORE, and the SCLC (the National Urban League was included in summit meetings but was primarily an organization engaged in behind-the-scenes philanthropic activities for blacks). The movement also included a network of church and labor activists (e.g., A. Philip Randolph's Negro American Labor Council, the initial sponsor of the famed 1963 March on Washington). With the passage of the 1964 and 1965 civil rights acts, regarding public accommodations and voting rights, the caste status of blacks was slowly changing due to the destruction of the country's racist legal structure. The main objectives articulated since the end of the Civil War, equal rights and social integration, had been achieved. Yet there was still unfinished business: economics.

King, Randolph, and others, however, were beginning to shift their focus from the South to black enclaves outside of it, in the North and other parts of the nation. With the Watts riots (a.k.a. "the rebellion") of 1965, the nation, including King himself, was waking up to the fact that the patient mood of the Negro masses, as articulated in the SCLC's philosophy of nonviolence and racial reconciliation, was becoming tenuous. This tenuousness was also expressed in the fraying of the coalition among the four operational civil rights organizations over the previous ten years. These organizations, with different orientations, had always cooperated, and yet they had also always been in competition with each other.[3]

(It is interesting to note that when the Kerner Commission's *Report of the National Advisory Commission on Civil Disorders* mentioned the different styles of these organizations, the NAACP was described as having the most "varied programs" while SNCC was dismissed as "living on subsistence allowances," a group that made "going to jail a way of life." Might this description have something to do with the fact that the NAACP's executive director, Roy Wilkins, was the only civil rights leader (and the second of only two blacks out of eleven) on the commission?)

Also, given HNIC Syndrome, some blacks had no qualms about using strong-arm tactics against others. A case in point is Adam Clayton Powell, Jr. who threatened to falsely accuse King of being involved in a tryst with Bayard Rustin, who was gay.[4]

As the nation's oldest civil rights organization, and the

most conservative, the NAACP had been wary of King's more confrontational, albeit nonviolent, approach, preferring to use the courts and lobbying, which it had done for about fifty years with limited success. However, King, the SCLC, SNCC, CORE, and others, along with the NAACP, had gotten the country to confront the issue of race and eradicate the most egregious segregationist barriers within a mere *ten* years, from 1955 to 1965. Arguably, had the direct action movement not come along, the NAACP would still have been plodding through the courts with the same mixed results: laws on the books but no actual improvement in the lives of blacks. King, consciously or not, had come upon a winning formula: out-side pressure—direct action, boycotts, moral suasion, etc., through organizations like the SCLC and SNCC—and inside negotiators or lobbyists, like the NAACP and the National Urban League.

But by the mid-1960s the times had changed. Even though Malcolm X was gone, the Watts rebellion, songs like James Brown's *Papa's Got A Brand New Bag*, and the emergence of new heroes like Muhammad Ali made some blacks more aware, more assertive, and angrier about their condition. Carmichael, the more militant members of SNCC, and younger blacks in general were finished with redemptive suffering; Carmichael himself had seen how Johnson tried to foist a bogus compro-mise on the Mississippi Freedom Democratic Party in Atlantic City in 1964 during the Democratic Party national convention. Now was the time for the emergence of a new black man.

Carmichael needed to isolate King from the conservative wing of the movement, the NAACP and the Urban League, and force him to take a position on Black Power.[5] Carmichael's move was both strategic and Oedipal. Black Power could become more pervasive if King endorsed it; it would signal a more radical orientation, a turn from civil rights to black liberation. SNCC, also had to "kill the father," so to speak; symbolically, King represented the more accommodating mainstream civil rights movement, and SNCC had to go its own way.

The marchers had reached Greenwood, Mississippi and Carmichael and two SNCC activists, Robert Smith and Bruce Baines, were arrested for trespassing when they refused to leave a black schoolyard set up as an overnight camp. King had left the march for a few days to attend other matters, and returned later. Released hours later, Carmichael, a lanky New Yorker by way of Trinidad, climbed up on a flatbed truck and told the audience that "every courthouse in Mississippi should be burnt down tomorrow so we can get rid of the dirt." He argued that black sheriffs should be running the Delta counties and that black people ought to demand something new: "black power." As King biographer David Garrow wrote:

> "We want black power," [Carmichael] shouted and the crowd took up the chant: "We want black power. We want black power." Although Friday's news account paid the new phrase little heed, the marchers knew that the divisions that had plagued them since the onset of the March has now been given a name.[6]

After returning to the march, King took issue with the new slogan. He found it divisive, but had no quarrel if

Carmichael or CORE's Floyd McKissick used the terms "black consciousness" or "black equality." King feared that with the other term, "whites would read intimations of black separatism and violence into the phrase . . ."[7] Black Power signaled a rupture within the civil rights coalition, for mainstream consensus organizations like the NAACP and the Urban League would have no truck with it. To a certain degree, the movement, as it had been known since the late-1950s and early 1960s, was over, and the various elements of the coalition would go their own ways. The NAACP would continue its lobbying and legal work. Both CORE and SNCC would become more radical in their pronouncement of black power, but only CORE would remain flexible enough to obtain funds to do urban poverty work. The SCLC would begin its slow decline into operational confusion. Its lasting epitaph would be King's death within two years of the announcement of Black Power.

The years 1965–66 were the beginning of a transitional period for the civil rights movement, the beginning of the end of "America in the King era," as Taylor Branch termed his two volume book on the period. The nation was experiencing increasing urban unrest; civil rights was losing its cachet as "Black Power" became a rallying cry that chased away liberal whites who decided to focus on another national problem: Vietnam. Yet Black Power was not the first red flare signifying a change in tactics or philosophical orientation of the black movement. Rustin had argued in 1965 that the movement had to move from the streets to the suites in his *Commentary* article, "From Protest to Politics: The Future of the Civil

Rights Movement." Even more so, no understanding of that transitional period or of the era of black liberation struggle can be understood without an assessment of the influence of the man that history would like to forget, Malcolm X.

THE BLACK REVOLUTION VERSUS THE NEGRO REVOLUTION: MALCOLM X

Malcolm X and Elijah Muhammad's Nation of Islam (NOI) gave white America a begrudging choice: it could either confront its history of racism and live up to its creed of being an egalitarian nation of equal opportunity, or deal with the likes of them. Paradoxically, while white Americans may have feared the NOI and its "white devils" rhetoric, the NOI was not in anyway a systemic or systematic challenge to white supremacy, except rhetorically and psychologically. King, on the other hand, was pushing the country toward a policy of economic redistribution after achieving the destruction of its racist legal foundation. In 1965, he told an audience in Philadelphia: "We need massive programs that will change the structure of American society so there will be a better distribution of the wealth."[8]

What unnerved white America about the NOI was its wild-card position in the body politic. Unlike King, who found whites redeemable through Christian love, the NOI white devilry school of thought unabashedly dismissed whites, and was quite explicit in saying so. Yet it was the Gandhian tactics of redemptive suffering and mass direct action that broke the back of apartheid America; the NOI essentially did nothing during the crucial civil rights period. It basically represented white America's deeply repressed fear of a black revolt, the fear of slave insurrection, and, finally, a fear of black retribution. It unnerved some whites that the vast majority of Negroes could actually be *thinking* the same thing as the NOI despite the profession of nonviolence by Negro leaders like King, and the urban riots of that period probably heightened white fear.

The NOI was (and still is) essentially a conservative organization. Taking issue with America's politics of racial subordination in regard to what the Nation termed the "so-called Negro," the NOI was politically apathetic during the entire civil rights movement while preaching its nostrum of moral reform, economic self-help, and separatism. As Claude Andrew Clegg noted in his exceptional biography on Elijah Muhammad, *An Original Man*: "The conservatism of the Muslims was a depoliticized phenomenon that was expressed through capitalist endeavors, the mythology of racial superiority, and monarchical/militaristic organizational structure."[9]

Muhammad, as the leader of the Nation of Islam— founded by Fard Muhammad in the 1930s—had also eschewed political activism due to his firsthand experience of being "indelibly influenced by the power of the state and its ability to censure and repress."[10] During WWII, he had been arrested and convicted for draft evasion and served a three-year prison term at the Federal Correctional Facility at Milan, Michigan, from 1943 to 1946. The NOI had survived its wilderness years of factionalism and persecution from the 1930s and experienced exponential growth during the 1950s and 1960s. This was due to its ability to offer a certain demographic of

African Americans a way and explanation of life that the civil rights movement could not, but also due to Muhammad's selection of a certain enterprising adherent, namely Malcolm Little, better known as Malcolm X. As a "lean, towering man with fair skin and boyish countenance," wrote Clegg, "Malcolm had a natural, or at least exceptionally cultivated, gift for eloquence and was a tireless recruiter for the movement."[11]

> The demographic of the Nation reflected and bolstered [Malcolm's] appeal among the membership, which by 1960 was predominantly male and between the ages of seventeen and thirty-five. Even among the ministers, men of Malcolm's age and younger were becoming the norm, and some patterned their ministerial style after his [as did Louis Farrakhan.] In an era when television shaped people's perception of almost every public event and personality, the Nation could do little better than being represented by Malcolm X. His blistering debate performances and talk shows made adherents proud to be Muslims, and his bold critiques of white America from Harlem soapboxes made blacks discontented with being just so-called Negroes. Fishing in the grave and organizing were his favorite endeavors, but hypnotic orations and cold, hard logic were his specialties.[12]

As Muhammad's chief plenipotentiary, Malcolm put the NOI on the map as the main Black Nationalist counterweight to the civil rights movement during the King era. The NOI attacked the tactics and goals of the civil rights movement. Malcolm even went so far as to call King a "traitor" to black people when King could not be enticed to a meeting with the Messenger of Allah, Elijah Muhammad, to discuss integration.[13]

Yet Malcolm chafed under Muhammad's restrictions on the NOI's lack of involvement in the black political struggles of the era. The NOI's appeal and membership was the largest in cities outside the Deep South—Chicago, Detroit, New York, Los Angeles, Washington, D.C.—the very places that the Civil Rights Acts of 1964 and 1965 would have the least effect. However, the issue of economic justice or economic opportunity was more salient; hence the Nation's emphasis on economic development, "doing for self." Years later, black conservatives who advocated "self-help," disdaining so-called black dependency on government resources, would spin this philosophy on its head for the conservative agenda.

The NOI had also garnered a reputation for recruiting and reforming those black urban dwellers who had fallen by the wayside and been ignored by Northern black churches. Seen another way, the civil rights movement was very much a "regional" movement that sought to lift the onerous stigma of second-class citizenship and reduce violence and intimidation that had been addressed at politically disenfranchised Southern blacks. Conversely, the Nation had the ears of those Northern blacks who experienced the stigma of second-class citizenship through lack of employment and crowded living conditions in non–Southern cities, and who had been stripped of their familial cohesiveness derived from Southern black folkways. While King and Malcolm were addressing national issues of racism and disenfranchisement, they both were addressing more or less local constituencies with slightly different needs. Hence King's tactics of love and redemption through direct action made sense in a region where blacks were repressed and murdered with impunity; it was a tactical response for a regional movement with national implications. Northern black urban dwellers faced police brutality, however, not the kind of systemic terrorist activity carried out by the Klan in the South. The urban dispossessed faced different issues, issues that led to eight cities experiencing riots in a two-week period in July 1967.

Malcolm X articulated a line of argument that looked beyond civil rights; he argued for *black liberation*. Muhammad, his mentor, had resurrected the core identity of "blackness" as an ideological and cultural concern from which Malcolm built his argument. Like Marcus Garvey's United Negro Improvement Association of the 1920s, the NOI was organized around a concept of blackness that was more attractive to low-income blacks, the majority of the NOI's members and outside sympathizers, than to middle-class Negroes. If the likes of King and Wilkins were "race men" of the Negro school, meaning proud of being Negro but still desirous of integration and white acceptance, Muhammad and Malcolm were the more racialistic "race men" of another old school, namely black nationalism. In the eyes of some, they were considered racist insofar that they deemed every white a "devil." Yet because the civil right leaders had neglected "race men" ideology, fearful of being seen as "nationalistic"—as evidenced by their response to "black power"—they had no relationship to the Negro masses who were instinctively "race men and women" due to the omnipresent reality of being *identifiably* black in America. In effect, King and Wilkins had ceded that relationship to the NOI and to Malcolm. The NOI not only offered an identity based on blackness, heritage, economic self-help, and moral uplift, but, as Brotz observed, it also spoke to the black masses' need for "subjective fortification" that could only be obtained by having "one's own culture, conceived as national identity, religion and language."[14]

It is this desire for "subjective fortification" that would make certain aspects of Black Power nationalism appealing to numerous blacks regardless of class status. The legacy of Black Power nationalism would also make hip-hop music a powerful vehicle for post-soul, post-black liberation nationalism, yet it would also make the gangsta rap variant a controversial music form, displaying the best and worst of America's urban bantustans.

Malcolm's blistering critique of the civil rights movement lessened after he left the Nation of Islam in 1964. His main objection to the movement was its concern with civil rights more so than with human rights, which led the movement to be easily absorbed and manipulated by the white power structure, as evidenced by the black vote becoming a dependable adjunct to the Democratic Party. Malcolm was the intellectual architect of the black liberation movement that was born after the cry of Black Power. Prior to his death, some SNCC activists were gravitating toward Malcolm's view of American society as implacably racist.[15]

Yet because Malcolm was assassinated before he could

fully act upon his evolving ideas and nascent political program, outlined in his Organization of Afro-American Unity, his popular legacy may well be his fire-breathing rhetorical style, more so than a lasting institution or body of work. In effect, Malcolm's life was the main "text," meaning his ability to rise from being "a hoodlum, thief, dope peddler, pimp . . . to become the most dynamic leader of the Black Revolution," as the paperback cover to the Grove Press edition of *The Autobiography of Malcolm* X proclaimed. However, Malcolm's most significant legacy was his ability to make so-called Negroes re-evaluate themselves; he challenged them to become *black* people, to seek their destiny not as a subordinate people but as one of many who were seeking liberation like the peoples of Asia, Africa, and Latin America. During Malcolm's sojourns in Africa and the Middle East, he made efforts to "internationalize" the black freedom struggle by trying to get African and Arab nations to condemn the United States in international forums, which caused the U.S. State Department much consternation.[16]

Malcolm's articulation of a "black revolution," as opposed to the mainstream civil rights "Negro revolution," was based on the concept of nationalism, a nation of people controlling their destiny by controlling land.[17] In lieu of controlling land or a geographical expanse of territory, Malcolm argued for blacks controlling key institutions and activities within their communities. He articulated an economic, social, and political philosophy that he called black nationalism. The political philosophy of black nationalism was based on the idea that the blacks "should control the politics and the politicians in the black community" and that blacks should be "re-educated into the science of politics so [they] will know what politics is supposed to . . . bring." In economics, blacks would control the economy of their community. Like politics, it also meant re-educating the black population into the science of economics that would allow blacks to establish industries and businesses. Socially, black nationalism would tackle the problems of "vices, alcoholism, drug addiction" so that blacks themselves could raise the level of their communities.[18]

These ideas were a counterpoint to the civil rights movement program of integration and pacifism during the late 1950s and 1960s and were specifically aimed at black urban dwellers. Before a Detroit audience, in 1963, Malcolm said:

> You don't have a turn-the-other-cheek revolution. There's no such thing as a nonviolent revolution. The only kind of revolution that is nonviolent is the Negro revolution. The only revolution in which the goal is loving your enemy is the Negro revolution. It's the only revolution in which the goal is a desegregated lunch counter, a desegregated theater, a desegregated park, and a desegregated public toilet; you can sit down next to white folks—on the toilet. That's no revolution. Revolution is based on land. Land is the basis of all independence. Land is the basis of freedom, justice and equality.[19]

In the 1950s and 1960s, the Nation was portrayed as a fringe, black racist group. Yet this perception of marginality was challenged by a charismatic Malcolm who offered some blacks a more robust, masculine rhetorical critique of American society than the civil rights movement did. It was his blistering critique of white racism and the denouement of the civil rights movement, along with a demand for black controlled institutions, which led SNCC and others to reconsider their commitment to integration and nonviolence. In early 1965 Malcolm was assassinated, but his "style" of "telling it to the man" defined the era of Black Power. In short, he left behind a "Malcolmist ideology"[20] and a style that "combined the wisdom of book learning with the world of the streets."[21] However, the inability of the nationalists, whether cultural or revolutionary, to build upon and beyond a Malcolmist ideology as "style" would have a lasting effect on black politics, both nationalist and mainstream. It would usher in a regime of symbolic politics that would place a higher premium on appearance, performance, and rhetoric than on a programmatic approach to solving problems.

WHERE DO WE GO FROM HERE? THE MOVEMENT AT THE CROSSROADS

Within a week of signing the second landmark piece of civil rights legislation of the 1960s, the Voting Rights Act of 1965, Watts, a black neighborhood in Los Angeles, exploded. The riot that raged from August 11–17 of 1965 caught both America and the City of Angels by surprised. Los Angeles had been heralded as one of the best places for blacks—then Negroes—to find employment. Writer Theodore White had cited the city as a place that blacks could receive the "most decent treatment and . . . the best opportunity for housing," but others knew something else: that blacks and the police were headed for a conflict.[22] In the aftermath of the riot, 34 people had died; at least 1,000 were injured and nearly 4,000 were arrested.[23] Property damage was estimated to be as high as $100 million to $200 million.[24]

Despite the loss of life and property, even more incalculable damage had been done to the idea of nonviolence and to established—"responsible"—Negro leadership, men like Wilkins, Young, and especially King. Watts blew the lid off the notion of a Negro Revolution that Malcolm had scoffed at, but which had won the passage of the Civil Rights Acts of '64 and '65. Yet these legislative acts presented no significant institutional changes for low-income blacks. The conditions outside of the South, in the ghettoes of America, had yet to be addressed, and the Watts explosion proved, to a certain degree, that the movement was too late.

In 1965, King had been considering Chicago and was looking at the issue of ghetto stratification there and in other cities. He made visits to Chicago and other northern cities, including Philadelphia, Cleveland, and Washington, D.C. (Powell, however, let it be known to King that his presence wouldn't be welcomed in Harlem, the most famous of black enclaves.[25]) King told a Philadelphia audience that his northern tour was aimed at addressing serious domestic issues. He told the audience that "We need massive programs that will change the structure of American society so there will be a better distribution of the wealth."[26] That was on Sunday, August 1. Ten days later, en route to what he thought would be a brief rest in San Juan, Puerto Rico, he heard the news of the social explosion in Los Angeles. Days later, King arrived in L.A. and had a less than pleasant tête-a-tête with Mayor Sam Yorty. He was given a rude awakening when he met, on August 18th, with a group of 500 blacks at Westminister Neighborhood Association in the riot-torn section of the city. King was heckled and more or less dismissed when one of the attendees informed him that LAPD Chief William Parker and Mayor Yorty needed to be there more so than he. After all, "They're the ones responsible for what's going on here."[27]

King acknowledged that point, said he would try to get them there, and replied, "I know you will be courteous." But Gerald Horne noted that something else was going on.

> At that, the crowd roared with laughter. This was beyond the metier that Dr. King had honed in the Deep South. This was South L.A., which had a different history, a different demographic makeup, a different reality. It was a reality to which the traditional civil rights forces had not paid sufficient attention.[28]

King probably would have concurred with that assessment. The L.A. riot had a very dramatic impact on him, and he felt that Negro leadership, which included him, had "failed to take the civil rights movement to the masses of the people."[29] Later, he told Rustin that he had worked to get black people the right to eat hamburgers at integrated, public accommodations but felt that he now had to help them to get the money to buy them as well.[30] The riot, along with subsequent eruptions of urban unrest, drove home the point that there was a disconnection between black middle-class leadership and the urban black working class. As King and the SCLC headed north, they confronted intractable Northern resistance and racism. In a Chicago suburb, Cicero, they were pelted with rocks. And they stumbled politically when an agreement they had worked out with the city and the real estate establishment, in conjunction with the Chicago Freedom Movement, "did not give the movement anything of substance in exchange for halting the marches."[31]

King and the movement had reached an impasse. They had failed to deliver broad economic gains for low-income blacks. As well as losing white liberal support for the movement, SNCC became increasingly more radical, and the cities were wracked with violence. Black Power had essentially fragmented a movement that was running out of steam and had already won its greatest victories: the NAACP's successful *Brown v. Board of Education* before the Supreme Court in 1954; the Montgomery Bus Boycott; the March on Washington; King's Nobel Peace Prize; and the passage of the landmark civil rights legislation. The coalition that had consisted of SCLC, NAACP, SNCC, and CORE had allied itself in groups like the Council of Federated Organizations (COFO), which sought to channel funds to the various projects of the different groups in order to circumvent the scrutiny of parent organizations, foundations, and the government.[32] Squabbling over funds, the organizations joined the Council for United Civil Rights Leadership, an organization led by philanthropist Stephen Currier and encouraged by the Kennedy administration.[33] King told an inquirer who asked about a possible parting of the ways in the movement that he got the impression that the NAACP—with Wilkins miffed that the Meredith march hadn't focused on national legislative issues—"wouldn't mind a split because they think they are the only civil rights organization."[34] Given how SNCC has ceased to exist and both SCLC and CORE have slipped into irrelevancy, the NAACP *is* the only civil rights group in existence, though it now appears to be an adjunct of the Democratic Party. The secret of the organization's longevity is based on its central activities having been geared toward the courts and state and national legislative lobbying. In other words, moderate, nonthreatening activities.

While King and others were well aware of the enormous task of dealing with entrenched urban poverty, their lack of a coherent program and vehicle to confront the structural problems facing urban poverty left King doing his routine balancing act. As journalist Andrew Kopkind noted:

> On one side, he tells whites that he alone can control the ghettoes, if they support his work and give him goods to deliver; on the other side, he tells the black people presumably under his influence that rioting will get them nowhere and that he alone can give them what they want. It is a complicated game requiring consummate political skill, and although King abides by the rules, he has not been winning many points. Whites have ceased to believe him, or really to care; blacks hardly listen[35]

Since the NAACP was already an "insider" organization, that is, performing as a lobbying group and litigating matters through the judicial system, it had less to lose if the coalition members went their separate ways. It certainly wasn't going to entertain the behavior, ideas, and radical notions of SNCC's Black Power politics. It had already shown that it was ready to jettison those in the group who carried the tint of radicalism. During the McCarthy era, it dumped one of its very founders, Du Bois.[36]

The association's strength, and another reason for its longevity, is that unlike the SCLC, it is not a charismatic organization, dependent upon the agenda of one lone gifted individual such as King or Malcolm X. In other words, its program isn't based on Messiah-complex politics. *As we have stressed,* the black political tradition tends to be heavy on charismatics—Marcus Garvey, Elijah Muhammad, King, Malcolm X, Adam Clayton Powell, Jesse Jackson, Louis Farrakhan—but weak in terms of building and sustaining institutions. With the exception of the NAACP, historically black colleges, and the black church, black America has sustained very few institutions—think tanks, foundations, publishing houses, media—that can cultivate new talent and sustain a tradition of learning, activism, or critical inquiry. Arguably, blacks, even with limited resources, may have had a stronger black civil society in the segregationist era since, as stated earlier, critical black public affairs journals or radio and TV shows are virtually nonexistent today.

THE RISE AND FALL OF BLACK POWER NATIONALISM

During the early 1960s, the Kennedy administration wanted the debacle of the freedom rides off the front page. They wanted to shift public focus to less confrontational, decisively back-page activities: voter registration.[37] Carmichael argued that the "South's four million disenfranchised blacks might help offset" the loss of white Democratic votes. As a tactic and strategy for organizing black people, SNCC "couldn't refuse the offer."[38] This tactic was largely successful and marked the beginning of the rise of post-civil rights black elected officials; but it also led to the unquestioning absorption of the black vote into the Democratic Party. Carmichael was also front and center at the further manipulation of the Mississippi Freedom Democratic Party by the Democratic Party. The roots of SNCC's radical change were grounded in its constant dealings with white liberals, the cynicism of the Democratic Party, the fanatically entrenched racism of white southerners (who mostly became Republicans later) and SNCC's questioning Israel's relationship with the Palestinians. Even Malcolm X, in his classic attack on the "farce on Washington," saw how the Kennedy administration was trying to blunt the radical thrust of the "Negro revolution"—and SNCC was the tip of that arrow.

The downfall of SNCC, however, was that it could not reconcile its free-wheeling, anti-authoritarian structure of individualistic commitment to struggle and its willingness to go to the next phase of the black struggle, i.e., black liberation, without greater organizational discipline and programmatic focus. Like later black liberation organizations, SNCC became a victim of its own incoherent ideology and rhetoric. It advocated that blacks were an internally colonized people, similar to other Third World countries, yet it didn't have the organizational capability to engage in a movement of "national liberation." SNCC also understood that Black Power rhetoric had an unmistakable appeal for many discontented urban blacks. However, it had no programs or mechanism to harness urban black anger into a coherent political agenda.[39]

The great and admirable thing about SNCC was its willingness to go where action was needed and help ordinary black folk in places like Mississippi, Alabama, and Cambridge, Maryland. Whereas King's SCLC emphasized moral suasion and hit-and-run demonstrations, SNCC—a cadre of organizers rooted in local communities working jointly with home-grown local leaders—preferred direct-action organizing to press for desegregation and voting rights. They were the "outside agitators" constantly denounced by unreconstructed white Southerners who knew and understood "their" nigras better than any goddamn pointy-headed nigra intellectual.

Carmichael's cry of "Black Power" indelicately placed an issue on the table that neither whites nor "responsible" blacks wanted to address, namely *power*. Whites and blacks may have gotten upset that it upended the etiquette of the civil rights movement, but SNCC had begun to question the efficacy of civil rights legislation and alliances when masses of blacks in the South and Northern ghettoes were still trapped in second-class citizenship and poverty. Carmichael and SNCC realized the upshot of what was transpiring: blacks essentially had no real power if they had to appeal to white conscience or rely on the federal government. Hence they needed something that whites had, namely power—but a black version of it.

However, the cry of Black Power *without effective programs* was also a retreat from the kind of pivotal organizing work—voter registration, freedom schools, political mobilization—that SNCC had being carrying out in the bowels of the South. By encouraging a cult of the gun, which originally began as Malcolm X's legitimate call for black self-defense against racists' violence, Black Power nationalism also opened the floodgates to undisciplined, even violent forms of protest that militant groups were unequipped to control. As H. Rap Brown, a SNCC chairman, once said, "Violence is as American as cherry pie."

In places like Watts, Newark, and Detroit, urban blacks were showing what they meant by the slogan of Black Power. In the parlance of soul music, a cultural contemporary of Black Power, Papa had a brand-new bag. Yet Black Power advocates like Carmichael were powerless to defend blacks against state repression or channel black rage into a constructive political agenda. According to Carmichael, he had argued against the Black Panthers describing themselves as a "revolutionary vanguard" organization because it would bring the heat of the state on black youths—and it did.[40] The Panthers also lacked the social discipline of rural, church-based southern black America, where reaching for the gun isn't the first option but a last resort.

To a certain degree, opponents of the new nationalists, notably Bayard Rustin, were right in seeing Black Power as a cry of frustration, a throwing in of the towel in regard to programmatic endeavors that SNCC had been engaged in. Carmichael's 1967 book, *Black Power: The Politics of Liberation* (co-authored by political scientist Charles Hamilton), failed to articulate a plan or program beyond blacks banding together. Internally, SNCC was unable to control what it had started, since it had constantly veered between being an organization with some structure and one with none and no "leadership." As with most New Left organizations of that era, the latter tendency won out. Yet the irony was that some of SNCC's most audacious programs—the Mississippi Freedom Democratic Party and the Lowndes County Black Panther Party—were exactly the types of political endeavors that offered blacks something more than rhetoric, namely an *independent* political base in a pluralistic society. They gave blacks a taste of power and a vision of an alternative other than being supplicants to the white power structure. But the euphoria of Black Power rhetoric and the militants' association of the civil rights struggle with a form of national liberation, based on the writings of Frantz Fanon and the third world's revolt against imperialism, would give the militants an unwieldy analogy to base their theoretical premises on.

Black Power nationalism's weakness, particularly revolutionary nationalism, was its adherence to a Third World/colonialism model, inspired by Fanon's *The Wretched of the Earth*, that was questionably applicable to the black situation in America. Insofar as it could be argued that African Americans were victims of "domestic colonialism"—slavery, Jim Crow segregation, and second class citizenship—their ability to deal with the "settlers" (i.e., whites) was very restricted. Unlike the peoples of the Third World, who were still under the colonial yoke of European powers, African Americans were ostensibly citizens of the United States. Hence the politics of "national liberation" was problematic since blacks, as citizens, could be put down as insurrectionaries had they chosen to rise up like some Africans had against the English, French, Portuguese, and Afrikaner colonists and settlers. (One could, however, also argue that since blacks had obtained citizenship under the Fourteenth Amendment and the right to vote under the Fifteenth but steadfastly denied such rights until the 1960s, the United States, despite its democratic rhetoric, hadn't become a full fledged democratic republic until the civil rights era!)

Notwithstanding the rhetoric of "violence . . . as a cleansing force" that frees the native "from his inferiority complex and from his despair and inaction,"[41] blacks were not living in an undeveloped region of the world where they could run to the bush or to the mountains. After all, Frederick Jackson Turner had declared that the frontier had ended nearly a hundred years earlier. Blacks were residing in the most technologically advanced nation in the world, and while the United States was defeated by Vietnam, a third world nation, the circumstances of fighting a foreign foe in *his* native land is qualitatively different from containing insurrectionary violence against one fellow citizens in one's own homeland. Both SNCC and the Panthers, noted Dudziak in *Cold War Civil Rights*, had argued that "the movement for black power at home was part of an international struggle against imperialism." *The Battle of Algiers* was used as a "training" film during that period. The preferred method for that struggle was the gun, but given how the government viciously repressed the Black Panthers and other nationalistic organizations, the cult of the gun was, to borrow a euphemism from the Communist Party, a serious "error."

The riots of the 1960s—in Watts, Newark, Detroit, Washington, D.C., and other cities—were less than insurrections, although there was an elements of that in them. They were more "emotional" uprisings, a blowing off of steam. As SNCC historian Clayborne Carson noted:

> The uprisings failed to foster a strong enough sense of collective purpose to override the endemic selfish and vindictive motives that emerged in the outbursts of racial spite. Black urban rebellions were too short-lived to transform personal anger and frustration into a sustained political movement.[43]

Thus Black Power nationalism failed to offer programs or an ideology that could help blacks actually achieve power or channel the energy of rebellion into a concerted movement. Based on a misapplication of some of Fanon's theories, Black Power nationalism, as a "radical ideology," misinterpreted the world and left black nationalist politics mired more in rhetoric than in substance. Misreading the urban riots of inner-city blacks as the beginning of revolution, the militants recognized that a "large and growing proportion of black were attracted to the black power slogan, though interpreted it in many different ways."[44] Yet the kind of programs that SNCC had been organizing in the South—voter registration, political mobilizing, economic cooperatives—had been tossed aside for a third world, national-liberation model that had very little do with an African *American* reality. Arguably, Puerto Ricans, more so than blacks, had a greater claim on the third world, national-liberation model, since that island had been invaded and colonized by the United States in the aftermath of the Spanish-American War.

Black Power nationalism, particularly the cultural nationalism variant, was more successful in redirecting or reordering the psychology of blacks in challenging white dominance. Its greatest lasting legacies were black pride consciousness, cultural heritage, black studies, and a greater sense of political awareness. However, an unintended consequence has been a legacy of black orthodoxy based on narrow definitions of black identity via practices such as Kwanzaa, Afrocentrism and post-civil rights political culture. Despite the claim about these practices creating an "oppositional" framework, as espoused by some, neo-nationalists and critical race theorists such practices merely serve as a means to keep the "natives" happy with their own brand of mystification. Maulana Ron Karenga, the leader of the US organization (meaning us—blacks—against "them," whites), invented Kwanzaa, which is based on a "Zulu custom."[45] However, the vast majority of peoples of African descent in the New World are descendants of the peoples of *West* Africa. There, "the vast majority of slaving was carried on in an area of West Africa where civilization had reached its highest point on the continent, with the possible exception of Egypt."[46]

By the mid-1970s Black Power nationalism was a moot point. Despite attempts at "unity without uniformity," the nationalist agenda had floundered politically. There were a few attempts at creating a broad, unified political front by having the black liberationists, especially the cultural nationalists, via the efforts of Amiri Baraka, unify with the emerging national black political directorate that was forming at the local and federal levels. During the '70s, blacks held several national black political conventions which came to naught because, as Robert C. Smith observed:

> The black community is too ideologically diverse to operate for long in a single, all-inclusive organization capable of *representing the interests of the race in its relationships to whites or the larger external political order.*[47] (Italics in original.)

In the eyes of some, especially political theorists like Smith, the "immaturity" of the nationalists, who never challenged the black establishment on its own terms by competing in elections added to the problem of ideological irrelevance. The nationalists, scoffing at the idea that the American political system could ever work for blacks, never ran for office to demonstrate a mass base for their programs. By not doing so they couldn't hold black elected officials accountable and gain a measure of legitimacy by demonstrating mass support for an alternative concept of the black political struggle.[48] However, established and aspirants black politicos easily co-opted the rhetoric and symbols of Black Power.

The election of Jimmy Carter as president in 1976, aided by millions of black voters by way of the Voting Rights Act of 1965, could arguably be seen as a referendum on the political agenda of the nationalists. Likewise, the 1976 election validated a growing black political class, a new black elite or black bourgeiosie, which had been coming into existence since the early 1970s. The Panthers had been severely repressed by the state; organizations like US had begun to implode internally, and leading cultural nationalists like Amiri Baraka had become Marxist-Leninist.[49] Stokely Carmichael left the United States, became Kwame Ture, and "retired" to the "Motherland" until his death.

Even though Cornel West tried to map out, if you will, an Afro-American revolutionary Christianity, via black theology and Marxism ("a dialogical encounter between prophetic Afro-American Christian thought and progressive Marxist social analysis"[50]), black radical activism had run out of steam by the mid '70s and certainly had no response to the Republican risorgimento during the 1980s. That West and the academic left, the theoriocracy, started spouting theory during the Reagan-Bush years may well underscore how irrelevant the left and black radicalism had become. In other words, Marxism was dead, but theory, academic theory, was hot— and career enhancing. (West's signature book, *Prophesy Deliverance!*, was published in 1982).

The Negro Revolution had won, but at the price of black political independence. The civil rights movement morphed into a national political directorate (legislators and civil rights organizations) and, despite obtaining some civil right legislation, it was shown to be politically weak and incapable of protecting and projecting black interests when Carter lost to Ronald Reagan in 1980. Black leadership no longer sought to mobilize black voters beyond the realm of voting, as it had organized blacks during the '50s and '60s.

When the U.S. economy began changing in the 1970s from

an industrial base to an emerging information-based, technology-driven economy, inflation and wage depression, job losses, and increasing competition from foreign nations meant that although the economy continued to grow, benefits accrued at the top only. Equally whites were less inclined to tolerate redistributive programs—affirmative action, welfare, etc. They would begin to feel that they had "done enough for blacks," as evidenced by the disappearance of the most egregious forms of racism and caste status. One of the goals of the emerging Republican risorgimento was to limit an "activist" government—"starve the beast"—by cutting the kind of public spending that fueled New Deal and Great Society programs. "That means Social Security, Medicare, Medicaid—most of which gives citizens of the United States a safety net against economic misfortune," according to Paul Krugman.[51] And one needn't guess who tended most likely to be on the losing side of economic misfortune when times are bad in America.

Eschewing protest politics along with mass political mobilization, and having become a willing adjunct to the Democratic Party, black political power had become a booster rocket that was ready to be jettisoned at the slightest notice, especially when organizations like the Democratic Leadership Council came into being during the 1980s. Black leadership's inability to mobilize black voters gave rise, subsequently, to a freelance form of black leadership that used the legacy of the civil rights movement and the symbols of Black Power to promote itself over the interests of those voters, most noticeably in Jesse Jackson's presidential campaigns in 1984 and 1988.

Organizationally, the black Left no longer exists, save for operations like the anemic Black Radical Congress, which began more as *reaction* to the "success" of the Million Man March. Adding insult to injury, blacks began to slowly realize that just having civil rights wasn't enough; there had to be an economic component to freedom. After all, not having capital in a capitalist society means one is a political prisoner. However, what passes for a black left today doesn't address the problem of black economic development or wealth creation, not even as cooperative enterprises. That agenda has been ceded to Farrakhan and the Right's nostrums about "self-help," which is an updated version of Booker T. Washington's industrial education policy. The black and white Left's general hostility toward business and trade, and especially the demonization of black business,[52] has made it possible for the likes of Farrakhan, with his bean-pie capitalism, and Jackson, with his Wall Street Project, to advance economic agendas based on charisma and patronage. Yet the economic potential of black music has never been given thoughtful consideration, despite the incredible record of black creativity in that field.

Neither the nationalists nor the integrationists accomplished much in the way of promoting or discussing an economic agenda. The NAACP has essentially pursued a policy, as Cruse contends, of "non-economic liberalism," which means that "blacks had no supplementary economic program of their own" and that "black leadership in the civil rights organization had no economic program on behalf of its black constituency."[53] Integration, especially as formulated by the NAACP under white tutelage, was predicated on "racial adjustment" and as such locked blacks into an irrational policy in a marketplace society.

> In a society where the making of money, the eager search after profits, the entrepreneurial activity, the superexploitation of labor and natural resources, the ownership of land, the perfection of technology, the expansion of industry, and where the apotheosization of every financial scheme imaginable for individual enrichment (even organized crime) was worshiped, the American Negro was being advised by white liberals to waive any program of economic advancement as a matter of priorities.[54]

Blacks had, as they would do years later, unilaterally disarmed themselves: first economically and then politically.

This missing element is emblematic of one of the main problems within the African American intellectual tradition: black intellectuals have a tendency not to think strategically about what may happen in the future or beyond the orthodoxies of academic, mainstream, or conservative thinking. Thus neither wing of the 1960s black protest movement thought to organize around the issue of economic empowerment. When the integrationists did so, it was around the issue of "economic justice," or later around affirmative action. They didn't seem to think about what would happen to black businesses that had been successful in the segregated black economy. "No social movement of a protest nature," as Cruse has noted, "can survive or have any positive meaning unless it is at one and the same time a *political, economic* and *cultural* movement."[55] (emphasis in original)

Both the nationalists and the integrationists missed out on the salience of black music, which was later swallowed by the white-dominated record industry. While it is questionable whether blacks were a "colonized" people, one could well make an argument that blacks in music and sports had been "colonized," and that black activity—labor—had been channeled into the performative aspects within music and sports. In music, blacks were channeled into making music, though black ownership *and* profits were rare, with the exception of Motown and Stax. However, if there was someone who could have served as a possible model for what Cruse had advocated, understanding the black agenda in three important and related realms—politics, economics, and culture—it was Soul Brother Number One, James Brown.

THE POLITICS AND ECONOMICS OF SOUL POWER, OR "GOOD-FOOT" CAPITALISM AND BLACK AMERICA'S RHYTHM NATION

With grit, grace, and gravy, James Brown rewrote the groove of R&B and announced the arrival of a soulful glide to a new consciousness: colored people—Negroes—becoming *black* people. Brown did this through his music *and* attitude, which represented the folk ethos of the black working class, rural and urban, by way of *soul*. Soul delineated a specific social experience and time of black people, not merely a style of music or way of dressing. To borrow from one of the original thinkers in cultural studies, it represented a "structure of feeling."[1] Negroes became black people and then African Americans, experiencing the civil rights movement, the death of the Kennedys, Malcom X, King, the war in Vietnam, and the good, the bad, and the ugly of human existence in America. No one better represented this transformation than Soul Brother No. 1. (But soul, like black power, also lent itself to group mystification about black people's "essence," which allowed issues, ideas, and interests to be glossed over or ignored in the name of the "black community.")

Brown was not only one of the main sources of 1960s soul

music (Motown and Stax being the other two), but personified it and elevated it to an art form. His revolutionary reworking of black popular music—from R&B, soul, funk—has made him the most sampled artist in post-soul music, hip-hop. Arguably, if there were no James Brown, there would be no hip-hop. Brown's genius was that he stripped away melody and went back to the atavistic root of black music: rhythm. Brown's seminal songs of the mid- to late-1960s—"Papa's Got a Brand New Bag"; "I Got You (I Feel Good)"; "Cold Sweat"; "There Was A Time"; "I Got That Feelin'"; "Lickin' Stick, Lickin' Stick"; "Say It Loud: I'm Black and I'm Proud"; "Give It Up It Turnit A Loose"; "I Don't Want Nobody to Give Me Nothing (Open Up the Door, I'll Get It Myself)"—announced, simultaneously, the arrival of a new style of black popular music and ethos (funk), and proto-nationalist consciousness.

While Brown has been lauded as one of the most dynamic and influential performers and popular band leaders of mid- to late-twentieth century American popular music, his philosophy and agenda of trying to end the "economic slavery" of blacks has been overlooked. This is understandable, since Brown is better known as a performer than as an economic theorist or political philosopher. However, this section will argue and outline that Brown was as an *economic nationalist* in the tradition of Booker T. Washington, who once argued that "No race that has anything to contribute to the markets of the world is long in any degree ostracized." Washington, as he argued during his tenure as the reigning HNIC of the late nineteenth- and early-twentieth centuries, saw entrepreneurial capitalism as a safer means of achieving black advancement than agitating for political rights. Brown, too, was a proponent of entrepreneurialism, as evidenced by his company, James Brown Enterprises. As a recording artist he used "good-foot" capitalism to promote his "soul power" agenda of trying to end what he viewed as the economic slavery of blacks. What we are looking at, though, is *economic development* and *economic empowerment* through black music.

Like the Wizard of Tuskegee, Brown believed in using entrepreneurial capitalism as a means to push black advancement, as did Motown's Berry Gordy and Stax's Al Bell. Brown was a proto-nationalist, meaning that he was first and foremost conscious of himself as being a black man from the American South, who, to paraphrase Washington, grew up from *economic* slavery, the dirt-poor poverty of Georgia. He also understood that even though he was increasingly becoming a successful individual, he was still a member of an oppressed minority group. However, unlike Nation of Islam founder Elijah Muhammad or his best student, Malcolm X, Brown was not a separatist. Nor was he a militant like Stokely Carmichael or H. Rap Brown, men who preached black power. Soul Brother No. 1 was about "soul power," establishing businesses and encouraging young people to stay in school. Yet it should be understood that Brown is an entertainer, and the dictates of that profession require that one reach as broad an audience or market as possible. Being "political" or speaking out on issues was fraught with the possibility of alienating a new market, which he did when he produced one of the seminal political songs of that era, "Say It Loud: I'm Black and I'm Proud."

In a February 1969 issue of *Look* magazine, Brown was featured in an article titled "The Importance of Mr. James Brown," written by Thomas Barry. The Hardest Working Man in Show Business was described as a:

[R]anking black capitalist, directly employing 85 people to run his production office, two radio stations (only five of America's 528 "soul station" are black-owned), record company and real estate interests. His annual payroll is $1.1 million. Spending money to make money, he has used promotions to boost his road gross $450,000 in 1963 to $2.5 million in 1968 (of which ten percent went to local youth group or charities). Records, publishing and investments pyramided his total 1968 gross to $4.5 million. He is now worth well over $3 million, but is not sitting on it: four more radio stations and a chain of black managed restaurants are being planned.[2]

Soul Brother No. 1 even owned a $713,000 Lear jet. Brown presented an interesting mixture of "group-conscious nationalism" and entrepreneurial philosophy of the Booker T. Washington model: pulling oneself up by one's own bootstraps, yet extending a helping hand to others below. Brown also made concerted efforts to encourage young people to stay in school and get an education, producing a 1966 message song, "Don't Be a Dropout." Brown was committed to the concept of using "soul power" to build, learn, and earn.

"Get an education, because all of you can't make it the way

I did. If what should be done in this country, be done, you got to be ready."[3]

As popular as Brown was with black youths in America's urban bantustans, giving them an anthem with "Say It Loud—I'm Black and I'm Proud," he caused considerable ire with black militants like Stokely Carmichael and H. Rap Brown by entertaining U.S. troops in Vietnam. The nationalists' uttered the vague but emotionally resonant cry of "Black Power," but Brown, with his hit songs, wealth, and political stature *had* the power and flirted with such establishment figures as Hubert Humphrey and Richard Nixon.

Brown was a more legitimate and influential black leader than either Carmichael or the other Brown. He was the embodiment of the common black folk ethos—soul, the transformation of Negroes to black people via the changes he made in R&B and contact with "the people"—and was pursuing a black agenda of economic development, albeit by means of "good-foot" capitalism. He was, to a certain degree, de-legitimizing the very claims that some militants were making: that a black man can't advance in a white racist society. This also made him attractive to the white power elite. Brown himself was a potential HNIC, and was recognized as such by the white establishment, which was more astute about manipulating him than the other way around.

Brown, to certain degree, lived out the Du Boisian notion of "double consciousness," the awareness of being both an American and a Negro and the inherent tension between the two. Not only did he produce songs like "America is My

Home," but went to Vietnam to entertain American ser-vicemen during the Vietnam War, causing H. Rap Brown to refer to him as the "Roy Wilkins of the music world."[4] Yet Brown was also very adamant about his allegiance to black people, stating that he "was a racist when it comes to freedom. I can't rest until the black man in America is let out of jail, until his dollar's as good as the next man's."[5]

"To million of kids on the ghetto street corners," wrote Barry in the *Look* magazine article, "he is living proof that a black man can make it big—and still come back to listen to their troubles."[6]

As a recording artist, Brown stood to gain the greatest profitability by selling the most records to the widest audi-ence possible. He wasn't Soul Brother No. 1 merely because he articulated the soul ethos of black America; he sold mil-lions of records that placed him on the R&B charts and pop charts. However, unlike Motown, which sold a "pop" version of soul music or R&B to white audiences, Brown's visceral, gut-bucket singing and dynamic pyrotechnic dancing was the unalloyed *real* thing, representing the performative soul ethos of black America's Rhythm Nation. Always uncompro-mising, Brown's music changed over the years as he crafted a new R&B sound, but he did not dilute it, and by doing so he brought whites over to black people's music on *his* terms. Brown wanted a wider audience and was concerned about getting on the pop charts because that meant access to the mainstream and a white fan base. Brown's band had generally always been black, but he integrated it (first bringing in white bassist Tim Drummond). He also worked for white-owned

King records (a Cincinnati-based firm run by the bull-headed Syd Nathan). And he had formed a close personal working relationship with another white, Ben Bart, a man whom he called "Pops."

Yet this drive for a wider audience and his working relationships with whites did not preclude Brown from being concerned about the status of black people during the civil rights era. Given his social background as a poor black youth from the segregationist South with a limited education, Brown viewed education and ownership of businesses as the key to black emancipation. To a certain degree, Brown was articulating an overlooked or misplaced item on the civil rights movement's agenda, namely economics. While King and others of the civil rights era focused on voting rights and the destruction of segregation, little was said about the *economic* consequences of black second-class citizenship. While W.E.B. Du Bois was right in criticizing Washington's overemphasis on economics years before, Washington wasn't wrong in seeing economics as a necessary component to any agenda that geared itself toward integrating blacks as citizens in a market-driven economy. Du Bois himself later realized that a focus on economics was also needed, and it bears repeating again:

It is quite possible that it could never cover more than the smaller part of the economic activities of Negroes. Nevertheless, it is also possible that this smaller part could be so important and wield so much power that its influence upon the total economy of Negroes and the total industrial organization of the United States would be decisive for the great ends toward which the Negro moves.[7]

Music, to a certain degree, has been the "smaller part of the economic activities" of blacks that has had a profound influence on the American economy. When one considers how hip-hop, along with its fashion, style, and attitude, has become the preferred soundtrack for advertising, black music is having an even greater impact than ever before, nationally and internationally.[8]

However, the legacy of the Washington–Du Bois debate, this either-or paradigm, would have a profound consequence on black political culture; for it would seal off the ability of blacks to synthesize competing or apparently contradictory ideas. Blacks would be locked into an either-or proposition that made it untenable to think about or respect the ideas of competing philosophies or agendas.

James Brown's rise in the mid-'60s, as Soul Brother No. 1, gave him an audience, a platform that was equal to Martin Luther King's or Malcolm X's. Brown was an authentic leader, up from the grassroots, who literally danced and sang his way to prominence. He was called the Hardest Working Man in Show Business not solely because of his sweat, but because of his work ethic: 300 shows in a year. He was "The King of the One-Nighters." He was also amassing property (homes, a jet, clothes) and starting businesses, yet he persistently advocated that young people stay in school and complete their education. His education stance made him attractive as a "folk politician" to both Democrats and Republicans. Brown represented a kind of "cultural leadership" and the formation of a black economic strategy that writer Cruse theorized about in his book, *The Crisis of the Negro Intellectual*. Cruse argued that the cultural apparatus was an avenue that blacks could use to make the United States a racial democracy. While other intellectuals, black and white, have often scoffed at the possibility of a so-called black economy, Cruse countered that:

> The black economy is a myth only because a truly viable black economy does not exist. It does not exist simply because Negroes as a group never came together to create one, which does not mean that it would be a simple matter to create a black economy. But it could be done—with the aid of attributes the Negro has never developed, i.e., discipline, self-denial, cooperative organization, and knowledge of economic science.[9]

THE CULTURAL APPARATUS AND BLACK CAPITALISM DEBATE: HAROLD CRUSE AND *THE CRISIS OF THE NEGRO INTELLECTUAL*

James Brown was a possible test case example of Cruse's argument in *The Crisis of the Negro Intellectual* in regard to how the "cultural apparatus" could be used to pursue a black agenda. Cruse argued for the emerging black middle-class, along with creative intellectuals, to become a real bourgeoisie; that is, to assert itself and gain control over certain entities of black life that had been controlled by whites. For

Cruse, the cultural realm was the weakest spot in the body politic's armor because blacks had long been in that world as entertainers, but men like Brown and Motown's Berry Gordy had begun to amass enough wealth to begin buying components of the cultural communication infrastructure.[10] In Brown's case, it was radio stations, which are very important to a musician. Brown was able to do so because as an entertainer, on the famed "chitlin' circuit," he had entered into one of the very few career options for blacks. In other words, Brown used the back door of the culture apparatus— show business and the communication system—to become a power player.

Yet Brown's new position—and the fact that he chilled a potential riot in Boston and was brought in to do the same for an ongoing one in Washington D.C. in the aftermath of Martin Luther King's assassination—made him a pawn in the grander scheme of things. Brown's pro-business position was just the sort of thing that was open to manipulation. It led President Richard Nixon to proclaim: "What most of the militants are asking is not separation, but to be included—not as supplicants, but as owners, as entrepreneurs—to have a share of the wealth and a piece of the action."[11]

Brown, to the dismay of some of his black fans, endorsed Nixon's reelection and was left dangling in the wind when the IRS began calling after him for back taxes. Was this an isolated incident, his tax problem, or the result of Brown being seen as a potential black leader by the FBI's COINTELPRO and therefore in need of being contained?

In *Black Awakening in Capitalist America*, an analysis of the black capitalism agenda of the '60s era, Robert Allen critiqued Cruse's lack of evidence in regard to his argument regarding the cultural apparatus.

> The most serious flaw in Cruse's work is this failure to establish, by argument or evidence, his central thesis concerning the salience of the cultural apparatus and the projected cultural revolution. He evidences an unfortunate tendency to substitute rhetorical assertion for reasoned argument.[12]

To a certain degree, Allen is correct in that Cruse failed to provide such evidence, or a model. If Cruse is "elitist,"[13] as Allen contends, it is only by the fact that Cruse had a tendency to cite jazz as the black cultural form that has shaped American music. Yet more salient models were available in regard to the impact of black music on American society, namely James Brown and Motown. But these were "popular" forms of black music; in other words, commercial, not "artistic."

What Cruse was calling for, once again, was the development of a new black middle class that would fulfill its historical role, namely political *and* economic *and* cultural leadership that would address the concerns of the black masses, as well as its need for money and prestige. This was a continuation of a debate that had gone on between Booker T. Washington and W.E.B. Du Bois, namely what was the best ways to formulate a new middle class that would lead the black masses. The former opted for economics while the latter chose politics through the "talented tenth." Cruse, to his credit, was trying to synthesize the two men's ideas and add culture to the mix. Cruse, however, was highly critical of the black middle class, understanding that

> It is a class whose social policies are so inept it seeks civil rights without seeking group political power, and then demands economic equality in the integrated world without having striven to create any kind of ethnic economic base in the black world. It is a class that could not have the motivations to achieve these things because it fears being nationalistic.[14]

Given Brown's background, pro-black sentiment, and his success in the culture industry, he was a likely candidate for a role model if had he obtained an adviser like Cruse. Yet Brown, to coin Marvin Gaye, was also a stubborn kind of fellow who may have well rejected the kind of articulated agenda of Harold Cruse.

Allen himself, while criticizing black capitalism, doesn't even mention Brown or Motown's Berry Gordy in his book regarding the conflict between black capitalists and the black liberation movement. These men were making millions of dollars, the epitome of successful capitalists. Music is scarcely mentioned at all in his book—only as an African carry-over or a vehicle for nationalist sentiments.[15] As with most black leftists of a particular era, Allen did not consider music or culture as a serious realm of political or economic struggle (and black academics never paid much attention to it until they went to graduate school and read cultural studies and critical theory syllabi). After all, it is only "entertainment," but it is an aspect of the cultural apparatus that blacks had entered as entertainers. Some, like Brown and Gordy, were beginning to emerge as owners, and some had a nominally progressive outlook regarding problems facing blacks at the bottom of the well. Amiri Baraka announced at one of the first Black Power conferences (in Newark) that Brown was "black America's Number One poet," but that he lacked a leader.[16]

The truth of the matter was this: Brown was already a leader—a leader of Rhythm Nation (the music-making realm that exists in black America; its greatest practitioners tend to come from the black working and lower classes). But he was also man with a limited education who could have used some capable advisers to help him put his "soul power" vision into effect, and help him better manage his financial affairs. Cruse had begun to connect the dots between culture, economics, and politics, but Brown wasn't figured into the scheme of things despite the fact that he had a vision, a following, and, most important, money.

THE HARVARD REPORT AND THE NEO-COLONIZATION OF RHYTHM NATION (BLACK MUSIC)

By the late 1960s and early 1970s, the major record companies began noticing the impact that black music (soul) was having on the charts and on their profit margins. A few years after Allen's book was published in 1969, music recording executives at major labels began looking at the success of the Motown and Stax labels and asking themselves: Is black music profitable?

In the early '70s, CBS Records commissioned Harvard University Business School to analyze this question. The university's researchers returned with an affirmative answer and a tantalizing and insightful nugget:

> Soul music is one of the very few basic art forms which is indigenous to America, although its own roots may be traced to Africa. It has been and probably will continue to be a vital and influential force on contemporary music. And Soul is by no means a static music form. It too will change.[17]

The Harvard Report was the beginning of the "neo-colonization" of black music, and the commodification of black culture, into the dominant music industry. CBS Records began bringing in many new black acts and structured deals with Stax Records and Gamble and Huff's Philadelphia International Music. At the same time, however, Jim Stewart, the white founder of Stax Records, felt that the major labels had "devoured or wiped out" the independent distribution network.[18] Seeing the impact that black music was having on the music industry, Gamble organized the short-lived Black Music Association (BMA), an industry trade group that sought to give black music-makers and owners a voice. However, the BMA lasted less than ten years due to the lack of a viable organizational structure, the vicissitudes of the marketplace, and the organization's dependency on music-industry financing.[19]

The BMA also did not receive strong enough support from

black recording artists, despite the rhetoric of Black Power or black unity. This neo-colonization of black music talent would deprive blacks of needed economic resources, since by 2001 hip-hop alone was generating revenue of more than $1 billion dollars in a $14 billion domestic industry (and $40 billion internationally).[20] From a quarter to half of that industry's profits is based on black music forms, or inspired by black music (i.e., rock and roll). But established black leadership has never understood the political economy of black music, never understood the shift of cultural capital to culture *becoming* capital. They certainly did not understand the new "black noise" that became the soundtrack of urban America—a cash cow for the white-owned major labels.

In the late '70s and early '80s, the music industry suffered a major economic retrenchment that led to black music departments being dropped or incorporated into the major labels' other departments, along with a decrease in promotion money aimed at black acts. Motown, once an independent label, had ceased to exist as such and became a subsidiary of MCA's Universal in 1988, then was sold to other firms during a later era of mergers and acquisitions. Stax had ceased to exist due to a bankruptcy precipitated by economic strangulation by CBS Records and its former lender, Union Planters Bank.

Motown's change in circumstance was due to its owner's ambition to build a media empire—movies, films, electronic equipment manufacturing—without having the kind of capitalization that could sustain it, and by neglecting the distribution that could keep it independent. Also, Gordy had left

Detroit, the symbolic center of soul or "R&B" music, and neglected to nurture the next wave of black musical talent that came out black America, hip-hop. It was the smaller record companies that moved on hip-hop and made billions for the major labels. These moves also left Gordy unprepared for the fact that the larger recording labels, now owned by huge conglomerates, began buying up independent distribution networks. The industry learned that it could profit even more by merely distributing and marketing music rather than actually producing it, farming actual production out to independent labels that could not distribute music. This method of production mirrored what had been going on in other industries, like the auto industry, and was called "post-Fordism," in which production was farmed out.[21] In other words, independent labels like Russell Simmons's Def Jam would do the pioneering work of identifying and recruiting black talent, and a major, say, Universal, would buy it or enter into a "joint venture," blurring lines between outright ownership and independence (which allows it to skirt labor laws). Virtually no major hip-hop label can distribute its music independently without greasing the five fingers of the music industry.

When the music environment did experience an upswing, it was due to black music acts, like Michael Jackson or the rise of hip-hop. Black music acts were an increasingly dependable source of profits for the white-controlled recording industry, with unequal remuneration going to blacks. As black business historian Juliet Walker has written: "Despite their contribution in revitalizing the American recording industry and their numerous personal and financial achievements, blacks did not emerge as the principal beneficiaries of the crossover of black music into white markets."[22]

Blacks began looking for an appropriate term to describe their relationship between blacks and the music industry. The irony, however, was that when an organization did exist to address such inequities, as in the BMA, blacks did not adequately support it. Years later, when Michael Jackson was going through his problem with Sony, he said before a black audience, "We don't have the institutions we really should have."[23]

During the 1970s James Brown also began to experience a tectonic shift in his fortunes. After years of being on the King label, Brown left and took up with Polydor, a German label; it was an experience that left him very dissatisfied. Yet Brown was also plagued by tremendous tax liability that gutted his former empire. Despite ushering in the funk era, Brown was also the victim of shifting musical tastes, such as the rise of disco during the 1970s. Brown's declining stature was arguably due to bad management decisions and capital overextension. It may also have been the result of the government being used against him, both the IRS and the FBI. (Given the history of that era, this bears looking into.)

Brown's legacy as an entertainer is more recognized than his attempt to formulate an economic agenda to end black economic slavery. Intellectuals like Cruse had the theory, and Brown had the practice, yet neither were combined in any meaningful way that might have offered African Americans a model of economic development within a marketplace economy based on their own cultural practices. Neither Brown nor black music survived the end of the '70s as they began it; that is, in a state of relative independence. Brown may have lost his empire due to bad management practices and/or manipulation by the government. Motown, the flagship of black music, was absorbed into the white-controlled recording industry, and Stax had crashed by the mid-'70s. It wasn't until 1987 that the NAACP released the only report that was ever done by an ostensibly black organization, "The Discordant Sound of Music," but it was too late. Black music had been absorbed. The civil rights movement depended on black music artists to provide funds for the struggle, but never took an interest in it as a possible foundation for economic development. A new postmodern form of capitalism—based less on production, more on distribution—had begun to restructure the music industry, and black music's Rhythm Nation was an essential building block within the conglomerization of culture.

The rise and fall of the Rhythm Nation closely parallels the rise and fall of Black America. As we have shown, Black America rose within the historical context of the civil rights movement as black people began to define themselves as a nation within a nation, transforming themselves from Negroes to blacks to African Americans. While the middle-class component of the civil rights movement articulated a move toward integration, Malcolm X, SNCC and the various other ideologies of Black Power articulated a desire for something more than being chocolate-covered white people. However, the repressive powers of the state and Black

Power's own ideological confusion resulted in a limited Black Power agenda that was primarily restricted to the realm of culture practices like Kwanzaa or ethnic pride. Neither the nationalists nor the integrationists paid much attention to the economic potential of black America's unique cultural heritage, namely music. This neglect has had profound economic and political consequences: the incorporation of black music without blacks actually controlling it made blacks employees of their own music. In 2001, the sales figures for the entire black-owned entertainment industry, as detailed by *Black Enterprise* magazine, was $189.75 million. However, hip-hop alone generated $1.8 billion in sales,[24] but hip-hop, like all genres of the music industry, is firmly ensconced within and controlled by a white-dominated recording industry. Given the lack of capital and other impediments, blacks have a hard time gaining a foothold in the distribution nexus of the communication and cultural apparatus. Blacks, as consumers, spend $600–$700 billion in the United States, but black business receipts take in an estimated $90 billion. Even a successful businessman like Robert Johnson, the owner of BET, had to become a subsidiary of Sumner Redstone's Viacom in order to bloom and grow. Even when various individuals have the right business components, blacks have never succeeded in merging their businesses in such a way as to create a cultural economic entity that can't be ignored. Unlike CBS Records, which commissioned the Harvard Report to look at future trends within the music industry, blacks never understood that the ground was shifting beneath them, especially in regard to distribution. As

Cruse once argued: "Negro intellectuals produce . . . no original economic theorists who can cope realistically with either capitalism or socialism from a Negro point of view."[25]

Instead of understanding and explaining the hard aspects of culture and economic infrastructure, the black intelligentsia has opted to interpret the soft side—black pop culture. That neither black intellectuals nor black political leadership have ever really considered the *economic* potential of their own cultural heritage shows that blacks are still the victims of "[incompetent] radical social theory" and the continuing "default of the Negro intelligentsia."[26]

CHAPTER FIVE

NOTES ON THE NIGGARATI
OR, WHY DEAD WHITE MEN STILL RULE

O nce upon a time, not too long ago, a wise minister once pondered a paradox. How is it that black intellectuals over a hundred years ago— endowed with few resources, facing every imaginable form of racial disenfranchisement, living in a world of routine racist lynchings—conducted an intellectually serious program of cooperative and engaged research, focused on the basic life conditions of black Americans?

The Rev. Eugene Rivers, who posed this question, probably never received an adequate answer. Possibly frustrated at the posturing of so-called black public intellectuals and the do-nothingism of the civil rights industry, Rev. Rivers, concerned about the deteriorating lot of young blacks, signed onto the Bush administration's faith-based initiative. Rev. Rivers was decidedly *old school*; he wanted to improve the lot of urban bantustans by focusing on issues like employment, education, health, and spiritual impoverishment.

Today's black public intellectuals understand that if help is going to be extended it has to be done within the context of *culture*, something that an old schooler like Rivers wouldn't understand. The best way to assist in this program is to provide the mainstream with interpreters of the urban *cri de coeur* that is often at the center of hip-hop music and culture. To be sure, those who can best do this kind of intellectual work are those public intellectuals who have been trained by the universities' theoriocracy that has come to influence academic discourse. It's all about cultural criticism as a means of understanding the sinews of power that courses through the body politic and its culture.

Academic cultural criticism is the coin of the realm for a fair number of post-civil-rights-generation black intellectuals. Schooled in the humanities (literature, feminism, critical theory, cultural studies), it has produced Afro-literary theorists like Houston Baker (*Blues, Ideology, and African American Literature*) and Henry Louis Gates, Jr. (*The Signifying Monkey*), and oppositional critics such as Cornel West (*Prophesy Deliverance!*), bell hooks (*Black Looks*) and Michael Eric Dyson (*Reflecting Black*). This rising tide of voices has even lifted the profile of an old-school paradigmer (i.e., Marxist or neo–Marxist) such as Manning Marable (*How Capitalism Underdeveloped Black America*).

Some have risen to new heights: posted at elite universities (Yale, Harvard, Princeton, Columbia), fêted on television, sought after for knowledge about the black world or blackness, the recipients of large book and television contracts and positions on boards of prestigious institutions these intellectuals—some at least—are living large. The term public intellectuals, however, has been appropriated by some not in the pursuit of disseminating truly critical knowledge, as in the case of Noam Chomsky or the late Edward Said or

NOTES ON THE NIGGARATI

Christopher Hitchens, but as a means of presenting themselves as *market* intellectuals who interpret black culture for those too disenfranchised to speak for themselves.

This is made possible by the fact that the "public," so to speak, has ceased to exist and has been replaced by various discrete markets in a society that reduces everything to dollar signs. If by some chance black public intellectuals know nothing of the subject matter they are called upon to explain, that is a moot point. The point is they have engaged the public, which is usually white and has money.

Yet never have so many theorized about so much, while saying so little. Some have embraced the cause of hip-hop, which, to a certain degree, has made today's market intellectuals relevant. For beyond blackness and black issues, black market intellectuals have little to offer. The criticism of black intellectuals as being "frauds," "failures," or miseducated has been issued by the likes of Cruse, E. Franklin Frazier, and Carter G. Woodson. "The philosophy implicit in the Negro's folklore," wrote Frazier in his essay "The Failure of Negro Intellectuals," "is infinitely superior to the opportunistic philosophy of Negro intellectuals who want to save their jobs and enjoy material comforts."[1] Frazier also laid bare the shortcomings of the pre-civil rights black middle class in his classic, *Black Bourgeoisie*. Today's so-called oppositional black intellectuals are part and parcel of a new black bourgeoisie, making up a "niggarati," if you will. (A term, like pet Negro, coined by Zora Neale Hurston.)

Hip-hop, for better or for worse, has allowed some of the niggarati to bolster their black credentials before black

audiences and white markets. After all, if one is a black intellectual, particularly a black *market* intellectual posing as a *public*
intellectual (but functioning as a "native informant"), hip-
hop offers a chance to raise one's profile (and profit). However, black intellectuals have not, at least according to Cruse,
been able to "see the implications of cultural revolution as a
political demand growing out of the advent of mass communication media. Having no cultural philosophy of their own, they
remain under the tutelage of irrelevant white radical ideas."[2]
One only has to peruse some of the above titles to confirm
this view. Of course there is the usual spouting of "commodification," but, once again, this is refracted through Frankfurt
School critical theory, French continental theory or British
cultural studies. American intellectuals, both white and
black, have a theoriority complex.

Black "public" intellectuals have pimped off of hip-hop
rather than actually delineating how it is situated within the
political economy of the multi-billion-dollar music industry,
an industry that rests comfortably and unquestionably on
black talent. A case in point is Manning Marable's online essay
"The Politics of Hip Hop." In that article, Prof. Marable,
director of the Institute for Research for African American
Studies at Columbia University, performed the role of stenog-
rapher to Russell Simmons's Hip-Hop Summit Action Network (HSAN). The article was primarily a recitation of the
mogul's agenda (or initiative)—"the prison industrial complex,
the death penalty, voter education, and music censorship,"—
and a primer regarding the politics of hip-hop.[3]

Missing, however, was an analysis of how hip-hop,

particularly Simmons's brand, fits into the music industry. This is somewhat astounding considering that Professor Marable is the author of *How Capitalism Underdeveloped Black America*, which analyzed how the capitalist mode of production gutted black America. Motown is mentioned only once in the entire book, and that is in the accepted framework of black capitalism, which, according to Marable, has the possibility of pushing the "advocates of black capitalism into the political camp of the most racist and conservative forces of white America."[4]

Music for most market intellectuals is an afterthought, used as a means to end, and that end is seldom about understanding the entire political, economic, and cultural nexus of the various art forms that blacks have produced but have no real control over. Most independent rap record labels are partially owned by one of the five major labels—Time Warner, Sony Music, Bertelsmann Music Group, Vivendi/Universal, EMI—and serve as compradorian depots for the recruitment of young naïve artists who form a black Rhythm Nation that comes from the inner cities.

Issues such as the transparency of recording contracts, health benefits, work-for-hire clauses, and Internet royalties are not raised at most hip-hop summits, especially the ones formed by Simmons. The supreme irony is that white groups such as the Recording Artist Coalition and the Future of Music Coalition are beginning to organize around these bread-and-butter issues that affect all musicians. But these aren't supposedly *black* issues, and certainly not black *music* issues, which may oddly explain why the historically most exploited musicians are missing in action on music industry struggles.[5]

Black cultural criticism is a dubious enterprise. *Black Popular Culture*, a project organized by Michelle Wallace, introduced a truncated version of black culture: the book basically reduced black culture to two art/entertainment forms, namely hip-hop music and films. The book became the product of an allegedly black intellectual debate about culture that was, once again, refracted through the then-current theoretical prisms of "pleasure," identity politics, theory and cultural criticism. Another book, *Soul: Black Power, Politics and Pleasure*, edited by Monique Guillory and Richard C. Green, primarily treads over the same path. Yet mostly missing from these books is any sense that "black culture" or "soul" are defined by social, political, and economic environments which came out of a basic folk culture, an ethos based on a "structure of feeling" about a certain time and place in history. Usually an occasional academic from the social sciences is present, but one gets the impression that these cultural critics are high on the octane of questionable theoretical importance.

Given the lack of insight that black intellectuals have brought to rap, it's not too surprising that Michael Eric Dyson chose to write a book about Tupac Shakur (*Holler If You Hear Me*) that is part and parcel of the martyrdom hagiography that unfortunately defines African American political culture.

If, however, one wants a truly riveting interrogation of the cultural text of our time, one should read bell hooks's April 1997 interview of Lil' Kim in *Paper* magazine ("Hardcore Honeys"). hooks not only gets knee-deep but totally deep with the *faux* bad gal of hip-hop.

bh: What was your line on *Hardcore*, "take it up the butt"? Don't be funnin'. What do you think about that?

LK: I think it's real.

bh: Tell me what you mean when you say it's real— that a lot of people are getting fucked in the butt?

LK: Exactly . . .

And Kim wasn't speaking metaphorically, either. Later, hooks, supposedly a feminist, says this about her mother and the women of previous generations:

bh: My mother and other older generations felt that in exchange for the pussy, you should get marriage, you should get something. I'm not that kind of girl, though. I think real sexual liberation means that you're in charge of your pussy; you don't have to exchange it for anything.[6]

Whenever hooks tried to steer the interview toward Kim's persona being dictated solely by men or as a marketing gesture to male fantasy, girlfriend didn't completely swallow. If Kim doesn't have much to say about love (and she doesn't), hooks does in her latest work. To date, she has written three books about love: *Communion*, *All About Love*, and *Black Salvation*, as well as two books on black maculinity, *Real Cool:Black Men and Masculinity* and *The Will to Change: Men, Masculinity and Love.*. These books represent the Iyanla Vanzantization of bell hooks. It was only a short but logical hip-hop from "pussy" to "love," and hooks has followed Cornel West, her fellow intellectual poseur, to the zone of profitable marketability—the ultimate goal of market intellectuals—under the rubric of "cultural critic."

"In all modesty, this project constitutes a watershed moment in musical history," read West's website, touting his rap/spoken word collection, *Sketches of My Culture*. After listening to the CD one wonders if Lawrence Summers called West in for a conversation due to the hubristic nature of the CD rather than for it besmirching Harvard's good name. West, who has always sounded like a bad version of Richard Pryor doing a preacher, has produced a moment of profound afro-kitsch. Tracks such as "Stolen King," "Elevate Your View" and "3M's" (as well as the rest of the album) are nothing more than smooth "jazz" confections. *Sketches of My Culture* will easily find rotation on black radio stations during Black History Month, which has already been reduced to selling black tchotchkes (as in the case of Kwanzaa). In so many ways, West is representative of the paper-thin intellectual apparatus that is the hallmark of today's black intelligentsia.

The "tragedy" of West is that he has been seduced by the bitch-goddess of celebrity. Despite his alleged intellectual acuity and his status as an "intellectual freedom fighter," his output in the public sphere has been an embarrassment since *Race Matters*, which reads like a watered down version of King's last book, *Where Do We Go From Here?* However, no one, except those on the Right, would dare say so. West has had the opportunity to start a think tank that could really delve into, and offer practical solutions to, the myriad problems that face blacks, especially those at the bottom of America's well. Instead he has contemptuously offered trinkets such as a spoken-word CD, anemic analyses of the politically banal (where everyone is in "process,"), coauthored books where it's questionable if he has actually contributed anything other than his name, and support for the likes of Al Sharpton.

One suspects that he supports Sharpton because the reverend is thought to be an "authentic" leader, up from the people, while West and others like him are ensconced at white institutions. Hence his association with Sharpton provides him "black credentials." West supposedly is a "progressive," but he has been all over the political map, backing people such as Farrakhan, Bill Bradley, Sharpton and others. His sole criteria are always the same for any intellectual on the make as a hired gun: attaching oneself to a would-be philosopher-king or anyone who can rabble-rouse but still needs a reading list with West's books on it.

This uplifting, "elevating" project clearly answers what the minister at the beginning of this chapter was pondering. Black cultural criticism is merely a performance mode for "public" intellectuals who, while presenting their anemic offerings as discourse on subjects like hip-hop profit while they pretend to be prophets. Meanwhile, West's "business partner" Henry Louis Gates keeps an establishmentarian distance and builds an off-the-radar empire.[7]

Trained in the high falutin theoretical abstractions of academic feminism, cultural studies, semiotics, structuralism and post-structuralism, literary theory, and meta-theory, the niggarati may well be the most useless group of Negroes that black America has ever produced. None has yet matched the work of earlier generations: *Black Reconstruction* (Du Bois), *The Black Jacobins* (James), *The Betrayal of the Negro* (Logan), *Class, Caste and Race* (Cox), *The Mis-Education of the Negro* (Woodson), and *The Black Bourgeoisie* (Frazier). Cruse's *The Crisis of the Negro Intellectual* is the most searing indictment of the black intelligentsia to date—and it was written more than thirty years ago. Only obliquely mentioned or referred to by either black or white commentators during the "debate" about black intellectuals, *The Crisis of the Negro Intellectual* critiqued black intellectuals as being incapable of having an original thought. They either became superficially familiar with Marxism during the 1930s or mouthed the shopworn ideas of the dominant society in the 1960s, both replaced by left theoretical abstractions or Republican marketplace ideology. Their greatest failure has been their collective inability to develop a comprehensive view of the unique historical position of blacks in America, encompassing politics, culture, and economics.

Instead, they have readily subscribed to any half-baked theoretical construct devised by whites; and the academy since the late 1970s has been knee-deep in structuralism, Foucault, cultural studies, pop culture, etc., all of which has had a disastrous effect on the academic Left, the theoriocracy. Ensconced in the academy, the Left began talking to itself in an unintelligible language, promoting entirely self-referential concepts. Schooled in such language, charter members of the niggarati—Cornel West, Henry Louis Gates, Jr., Houston Baker, bell hooks, Michael Eric Dyson—were able to dazzle the white world with their mixture of "street" analysis and postmodern argot. West and Gates were allowed through the portals of Western civilization when West published *Race Matters*, a meretricious piece of social-democratic sop that pales in comparison to King's *Where Do We Go From Here?*, and when Gates addressed the purported rise in black anti-Semitism in the *New York Times* (challenged in Ishmael Reed's *Airing Dirty Laundry*; Reed asserts that the Anti-Defamation League had not found black anti-Semitism on the rise).

The civil rights era (or at least its results) has to be understood as having had the following effects: (1) it convinced whites that racism had ended, and (2) it severed black leadership—political, intellectual, and business—from the masses. The result was a large-scale payoff to the black elite and black intellectuals—left, center, and right—which would hardly lead them to question the efficacy of affirmative action. The fact is they have become a sliver of that 20 percent of the nation's population, cited by Christopher Lasch, that is indifferent to the fortunes of the other 80 percent.[8] Black elite support of Colin Powell in a *New Yorker* article is understandable.[9] As the most successful affirmative-action graduate, Powell legitimizes them and points out the irrelevance of the black Democratic Party elite.

Unbeknownst to most blacks, these intellectuals have hastened the quiet dismantling of black leadership and effective black politics. But an analysis of what happened is not forthcoming from the niggarati. As Manning Marable has said:

The new black public intellectuals . . . are engaged in

a totally different political enterprise. They are not building educational institutions like Tuskegee Institute, or political machines which negotiate for influence within the white establishment. They utilize power of words to impact the contours of political culture and public discourse. . . . [T]heir commitment is to theoretical and cultural engagement, analyzing the meaning of race, gender and class issues in the context of a post-civil rights reality of unrelenting attacks on affirmative action, welfare and multicultural education.[7]

Their "political enterprise," if one can indeed call it that, has nothing to do with people but with theory, identity, books, publications, journals, television appearances, assignments from elite journals read by whites, socialist confabs, etc. In reality, they engage in self-promotion masquerading as intellectual discourse, positioning themselves as market intellectuals. However, no real understanding of what's going on trickles down to average black people, since, as stated earlier, there is no real meaningful cultural communication apparatus that exist within black America. The niggarati aren't about politics in a land that, as Gore Vidal observed, doesn't have politics but elections. They are running a game, and a few people, such Adolph Reed and Leon Wieseltier, for different reasons, have called them on it.[11] Marable himself has noted that "Gates sees himself as something of an entrepreneur; he has extensive influence within foundation circles and inside the white media" and "embraces a social philosophy of inclusionist integration, appealing to the most liberal wing of white corporate and political power."[12] In other words, a racket—an intellectual racket, but still a racket. This is the game of both the niggarati and pet Negroes (Clarence Thomas, Shelby Steele, Stephen Carter, Armstrong Williams, Thomas Sowell, et al.): to get into the racket, make a killing, and claim it as the individual pursuit of excellence.

The niggarati made its appearance at about the same time that multiculturalism did and, like affirmative action, multiculturalism is another pet project of that clique. On the surface, the argument for greater inclusion and participation by blacks, Asians, Latinos, and other so-called people of color is laudable. But one can detect its self-serving nature: it allows the niggarati to promote themselves as interpreters of "their" fellow Others to people of pallor. One has only to read the scribbling that passes as discourse on rap and hip-hop to see how the term multiculturalism is as interchangeable as Benetton's colors. David Rieff has observed that while many academicians cited the emancipatory powers of multiculturalism during the go-go '80s, "the conditions of the poor, of working-class women, and of America's non-white citizens deteriorated dramatically."[13] The academic Left, both black and white, is only interested in talkin' theory, but the Right is interested in taking power.

The production of theory had become such a racket that David Lehman noted the following in his book on Paul de Man, *The Sign of the Times*:

A professor with a flair for showmanship once amused

his MLA audience by offering, for a fee, to convert any attempt at a critical essay into a publishable paper. It was hard to say whether the speaker was in jest; his project sounded eminently practical. So long as an essay makes the right noises—and these may be inserted by the hired manuscript-doctor—the content seems almost beside the point. A set of reoccurring code words needs to be sprinkled over the prose, like ketchup over French fries. The first sentence should feature *hegemony*; the second *itinerary* [or *genealogy*]; the third *foregrounding*; the fourth, *privilege* used as a verb (for example "the retrograde critic privileges the author"). There should be plenty of *de-* or *dis-* prefixes, beginning with *deconstruction* and *dismantling*, and as many *—ize* suffixes, such as *problematize, valorize, contextulize, totalize*. A good way to begin your discourse (you must always call it that) is with a nod toward Derrida, an allusion to de Man, and a determination to call into question some binary opposition or other. You are going to deconstruct the dichotomy of your choice: *male* and *female*, *nature* and *culture*, *center* and *periphery*, *speech* and *writing*, *presence* and *absence.* The reckless may opt for *truth* and *opinion*; the really reckless, for *truth* and *propaganda*; the semiotically-trained analyst of TV commercials may stick with *slender* and *fat*. Your task is to dismantle hierarchies and you do this by showing that the first term in any such set is implicitly—and unjustly—endorsed ("privileged") in Western philosophy . . . It would probably be a good idea to mention the "prison house of language," too. You must remind your readers that no escape from language is possible. Language has humanity in thrall; textuality is all.[14]

In other words, *template* theoretical production in which the right set of coded words could be dropped on any subject matter and be made as a "critical essay," which isn't really criticism but dry, sterile, technical rhetoric. This, in turn, has created a series of glib, media-oriented black public intellectuals more conversant with pop culture, race identity, and representation than with public policies that pertain to economics, politics, law, welfare, etc. This new breed was clearly delineated by Japanese novelist Haruki Murakami in his novel *The Wind-up Bird Chronicle*:

> . . . [I]f you paid close attention to what he was saying or had written, you knew that his words lacked consistency. They reflected no single worldview based on profound conviction. His was a world that he had fabricated by combining several one-dimensional systems of thought. He could rearrange the combination in an instant, as needed. These were ingenious—even artistic—intellectual permutations and combinations. But to me they amounted to nothing more than a game. If there was any consistency to his opinions, it was the consistent lack of consistency, and if he had a worldview, it was a view that proclaimed his lack of a worldview. But these very absences were what constituted his intellectual assets. Consistency and established

worldview were excess baggage in the intellectual mobile warfare that flared up in the mass media's tiny time segment, and it was his great advantage to be free of such things.[15]

Smaller wonder that some today are marketing books on black self-esteem, love, or why they love black women. All one has to do is turn on the radio and listen to the *Tavis Smiley Show* with Cornel West and Michael Eric Dyson posing as "important social thinkers." Following this scheme of things, the black intellectual class has totally abandoned its social and intellectual responsibilities. Socially, emotionally, politically, and spatially removed from the day-to-day concerns of ordinary blacks, it is as remote as most whites are from blacks. The niggarati and pet Negroes have no interest in establishing or strengthening black institutions. There is no prestige or money at Moorehouse, Howard, or Jackson State that can rival or compete with Harvard, Yale, Columbia, Princeton, or Stanford, or any conservative think tank.

Since the election of Ronald Reagan and the emergence of the New Right, signs have been posted along the political terrain indicating that black gains were under threat, but black leadership—intellectual and political—failed to heed the warnings. Suffering from "African amnesia," African American leadership failed to recognize that the nation was shifting to an inhospitable period that paralleled the Reconstruction and post–Reconstruction eras. Historical works such as *Black Reconstruction* and *Betrayal of the Negro* chronicled the deals that led to the disfranchisement and the lynching of blacks. The crime is that the niggarati, intoxicated with deep theory, have no use for history, or for providing blacks with a social analysis of the forces arrayed against them. Instead, they offer treatises on the hybrid nature of identity or the Foucaldian "nature" of power. Let them study theory . . . African American intellectual "leadership" has been in a meltdown since the civil rights days. The drive toward integration has resulted in affirmative action for the aspiring middle class and welfare for the poor, but luckily only one has been on the chopping block, namely welfare.

Black intellectuals, particularly the niggarati, have never viewed black in-group economic development as a necessity for group advancement (and group protection), for that would be nationalistic ("essentialist") and capitalistic. Neither West nor Gates has shown much sympathy for that track. They have gained much more as beneficiaries of an elite patronage system that needs a smattering of dark faces to legitimize the rhetoric of meritocracy. Gates's relationship, as Marable noted, with the "most liberal wing of white corporate and political power" mirrors the old corporate dependency program of the NAACP, and we all know how relevant that organization is. Gates probably does not aspire to play the role of "a popular race leader"; he is successful as a race entrepreneur, a Booker T. for the 2000s and beyond.

Attributing the decline of inner cities to nihilism, as West does, is no different from the sort of condemnation heard from white and black conservatives, neoconservatives, and neo-liberals. West, like Gates, is far more comfortable dealing with whites and addressing their concerns than those of blacks, ostensibly his people. His book with Michael Lerner (editor of *Tikkun* magazine) *Jews and Blacks: Let the Healing Begin*, shows how utterly bankrupt the niggarati have become. It takes no great courage for West to speak to progressive Jews of his class, but he would be a real *mensch* if he talked to the Crown Heights Hassidim. This so-called intellectual risks nothing. (He also supported Louis Farrakhan's Million Man March due to "black operational unity.") Both West and Gates know that to become influential, they have to become "court Negroes" (as some Jews were "court Jews" during the era of European monarchies). The role of court blacks at Harvard is not to challenge power, as Noam Chomsky does, but to act as agents for a discredited policy that only benefits a few at the expense of the many. To paraphrase a biting comment once made about a Harlem Renaissance poet: these people are not thinkers, but nobody would dream of reproaching them for it, because, on the contrary, they possess an extraordinary faculty for defining the confused sensations that constitute the collective conscience of simple minds.

The black elite is the only parvenu class that expects to ascend to power through moral suasion. But considering whites' constant state of denial regarding race, it ought to have been clear years ago that programs such as affirmative action would only be a window of opportunity for developing parallel black institutions controlled by blacks themselves and thus not at the mercy of white mood swings. The comprador mentality of black intellectuals, however, prevented them from seeing beyond integration and the false foundation of the new black middle class. Even Du Bois, the patron saint of black "public" intellectuals, reconsidered his pro-integrationist philosophy in light of the Depression, arguing that blacks might have to engage in self-segregation in order to address the problem of group economics within a market society. Because of that, he was driven out of the NAACP. It should be no surprise that Farrakhan has a degree of credibility with some blacks: he *talks* about black self-empowerment through economic cooperation—with an emphasis on talk. Despite his limitations as a strategic thinker, Malcolm X, as a student of Elijah Muhammad, understood that black liberation would have to come through the development and control of black institutions. That is not a project that merits the attention of the niggarati.

Today's black intellectuals are prime examples of what Frazier saw as a drive toward dominant beliefs and values, an unconscious striving toward middle-class assimilation.[16] But the niggarati does it under the cover of so-called radical social theory. Except for West's departure from Harvard, this class of intellectuals has not produced any controversial ideas or theories. As matter of fact, if one reads the paper of record, the *New York Times*, theory is dead, but the power of ideas and philosophy continues as a project of the Right.

The Death of Theory and the Triumph of Straussian Shadow Intellectuals

According to an April 19th 2003 *New York Times* article, "The Latest Theory Is That Theory Doesn't Matter," a panel of the theoriocracy assembled at the behest of *Critical Inquiry*, academia's most prestigious theory journal, at the University of Chicago. "Leftist politics with which literary theorists have traditionally been associated have taken a beating," wrote the *Times*, and the panel was about resuscitating it.[17] This panel included the usual suspects: Henry Louis Gates Jr., Homi Bhabha, Stanley Fish, Fredric Jameson, and others.

W. J. T. Mitchell, the journal's editor and a professor of English and art history at Chicago, told the audience, "We want to be the Starship Enterprise of criticism and theory."[18] However, a student scuttled that project when he fired a laser torpedo: he asked what good was theory and criticism if the actions of Noam Chomsky were more important? The student, according to the *Times*, cited that Fish himself, in *Critical Inquiry*, had argued that philosophy did not matter.

Sander L. Gilman, a professor at the University of Illinois at Chicago, said: "I would make the argument that most criticism—and I would include Noam Chomsky in this—is a poison pill. I think one must be careful in assuming that intellectuals have some kind of insight. In fact, if the track record of intellectuals is any indication, not only have intellectuals been wrong almost all of the time, but they have been wrong in corrosive and destructive ways."[19]

Fish concurred: "I like what that man said. I wish to deny the effectiveness of intellectual work. And especially, I always wish to counsel people against the decision to go into the academy because they hope to be effective beyond it."[20]

Homi Bhabha advocated that some poems are "intimately linked with political oppositional movements," drawing "people together people in acts of resistance."[21]

However, Henry Louis Gates, Jr., stated that he really

didn't see "the liberation of people of color because of deconstruction or poststructuralism."[22] Sniffing the winds of change, Gates subtly distanced himself from the notion that theory matters. Now, for him, it's more about "institutional building"[23]—but Gates, an updated version of a Booker T. Washington-type HNIC at Harvard's Du Bois Institute, originally used such in launching his academic/entrepreneurial career. Once ensconced at Harvard, however, he used his position to become a "vital center" public intellectual who advocated "muscular humanism."[24] A "master of the intellectual dodge" in academia, Gates would make Machiavelli proud as a postmodern prince.[25]

The Chicago assemblage was, in fact, the end of the academic left's love affair with theory due to exhaustion, unintelligibility, cynical careerism, and departmental-budget constraints. It may also have something to do with a reality factor. A scholar/activist like Noam Chomsky, a linguist, doesn't theorize about the world through the texts of gender, race, identity politics via psychoanalysis, structuralism, Marxism, deconstruction, or post-colonialism, but examines the power relationships and policies of historical and present actors—nations, individuals, corporations, and governments; in other words, *real* politics.

Interestingly, the Chicago panel was held at the very same institution that gave birth to an intellectual orientation which has led to the dynamic and innovative ascendancy of the conservative movement. In the aftermath of the fall of Iraq, the French journal *Le Monde* ran an article, "The Strategist and The Philosopher," that looked at two men who formed the intellectual foundation of the Bush strategists and theorists who sold the nation the war on Iraq, Alfred Wohlstetter and Leo Strauss. Strauss taught at Chicago. While theory may be dead to an opportunistic theoriocracy, philosophy and ideas—the *right* ideas—have always mattered to Strauss and his disciples, the Straussians.

Strauss and his disciples are the individuals who have brought the American people the war in Iraq and the policies of preemption and an assertive, neo-imperialist foreign policy: William Kristol, Paul Wolfowitz, Richard Perle (he and others in the Bush administration may have Likud party connections),[26] and other officials of the Reagan and Bush administrations, including Seth Copsey, John T. Agresto, Carnes Lord, Alan Keyes, Clarence Thomas, William Bennett, and Robert Bork.[27] They are also scholars and writers such as Harry V. Jaffa (who wrote speeches for Barry Goldwater), Joseph Cropsey, Allan Bloom (*The Closing of the American Mind*), Harvey Mansfield, Willmoore Kendall, and Irving Kristol.

And because the academic Left has spent the last thirty years or so swilling theory, the disciples of Leo Strauss have embarked on a project—aided by corporations that have funded conservative foundations in conjunction with the religious right—that some have called "sinister."[28] They hold very elitist and pernicious views of humanity and American society, which have profound implications for American democracy and the world.

LEO STRUASS AND THE SERIOUS BUSINESS OF PHILOSOPHY

In the 1930s, Leo Strauss, a German Jewish émigré, arrived in the United States shortly after Hitler ascended to power in Germany, which left a profound effect on him. A scholar and intellectual, his field was philosophy; he was a Platonist with a keen interest in the history of political philosophy. Strauss taught at several American universities and colleges, but his real reign and tutelage was at the University of Chicago. Shadia B. Drury, a University of Regina professor of politics and the author of two books on Strauss (*Leo Strauss and the American Right* and *The Political Ideas of Leo Strauss*), has cited others as saying that Strauss's effect on academic life has been something of a phenomenon, producing the largest academic movement in North America.[29]

Yet if this is true, why hasn't one heard of him in this era of grand theoretical paradigms? Two reasons: 1) Strauss was interested in premodern philosophy, in other words, the views of Dead White Men; 2) Strauss also felt that philosophy was such serious business it had to be done secretively and in code. Strauss, in other words, did not trust ordinary and common people to understand philosophy because it would expose them to the sordid truths of reality, namely that there is no God. However, Strauss believed that the masses needed religion and nationalism—"noble lies"—to keep them and civilization from falling into nihilism. Whereas Marx once said "Religion is the sigh of the oppressed creature, the heart of a heartless world. It is the opium of the people," Strauss believed that the people *need* their opium. Philosophy was only for tough-minded prophets like himself and others who understood the wisdom of the ancients. Strauss also went against the grain. While the American academic tendency has been to establish value-free "political science" programs, Strauss emphasized the timeless and value-based wisdom of the premodern philosophers.

Strauss, who experienced the downfall of the Weimar Republic and the rise of the Nazis, was preoccupied with nihilism, which he attributed to liberalism, the Frankenstein of the Enlightenment. To Strauss, the ancient world was based on a natural hierarchy of aristocrats and subordinates who knew their stations in a world aided by religion and tradition, guided by those who understood the wisdom of the ancients. Some people, as Plato surmised, are "gold," while others are "silver" or "bronze." In a word, *inequality*. Liberalism upset that world because it was based on a philosophy of individuals pursuing their own somewhat restrained interests that tended to be short of virtuous. Put another way, bourgeois humanity was atomized, unrestrained, and bereft of God in a modern world that was technologically driven. Searching for answers, modern humanity might gravitate toward those with nihilistic proclivities: Nazism, communism, or liberal democracy.

Strauss, surprisingly, had a problem with American liberal democracy. He had transplanted his experience with his former country's failure with democracy to the United States. Though not perfect, the U.S. has a tradition of democratic institutions and processes. For Strauss, however, America was a pre-eminently modern nation, and that meant it, too, was headed for nihilism. "His prophecy was fulfilled by the ignominious collapse of the liberal establishment," wrote Karl Jahn, "both political and academic, in the face of the New

Left," during the 1960s and 1970s.[30] Strauss's philosophical pre-disposition was also driven by a sense of doom or crisis, which stemmed from, once again, his experience with Germany and the prevalence of European anti–Semitism. However, his view of a rotting liberal society and of an imminent collapse also informs the urgency of today's conservatives, who see the decline of America civilization due to pregnant fifteen-year-olds. Another feature of Strauss's philosophy is a friend-or-foe dichotomy: in the realm of politics, is it okay to kill one's enemy. If that's impermissible, treating him as the *other*, or as an alien, outside the code of normal conduct, will suffice. This view is commonplace within conservative politics, where the loyal opposition does not exist and the politics of demonization establishes the rules of engagement. One only need to recall that Newt Gingrich once termed the Clinton administration "the enemy of normal Americans," or the charge of "treason" hurled by one of many interchangeable blonde, leggy, svelte propagandists of the Right.

STRAUSS'S LEGACY

In *Leo Strauss and the American Right*, Drury noted several dom-inant themes that course through Strauss's philosophy: importance of religion; necessity of nationalism; language of nihilism; sense of crisis; friend-or-foe dichotomy; hostility towards women; rejection of modernity; nostalgia for the past; abhorrence of liberalism. Strauss offered his disciples something that the theoriocracy doesn't: a *Weltanschauung*, a comprehensive concept of the world and humans' relation-ship to it. To varying degrees, all of Strauss's dominant themes appear in neoconservatism and in some aspects of the conservative movement. Yet there is a social base and a fault line in regard to these two wings of conservatism that share these conservative tendencies. Neoconservatives tend to be Jewish and former liberal Democrats or Marxists, while the conservative movement tends to be non–Jewish—nativist, if you will—and was forged in the crucible of the 1964 Goldwater campaign and came to prominence during the Reagan years. The religious Right, Protestant–based, is one of the more prominent aspects of the conservative movement.

Neoconservatives also tend to be intellectuals who are academic scholars, think-tank intellectuals or government policy officials, while the conservative movement tends to be made up of intellectuals, religious leaders, office holders, and rank-and-file true believers. The neocons and conservatives' relationship with Israel is purely of political and Biblical convenience. It has more to do with the former wanting Israel to be safe and secure as the dominant power in the Middle East, while conservatives, who still want to Christianize Jews, believe the presence of Israel will bring forth Armageddon and a rapture that will bring the righteous—those believing in Christ, of course—to heaven. The Israelis, along with AIPAC, can count on the religious Right's base in the GOP to make sure that Bush will not press Israel to make concessions to the Palestinians.

Strauss died in 1973. However, his pervasive influence has lived on through his students, such as Allan Bloom, Harvey Mansfield, Harry Jaffa, and others in academia, and in the realm of politics through the rise of the neoconservative movement, best exemplified by Irving Kristol and now William Kristol, the editor of the *Weekly Standard*. In reality, neoconservatism has become the dominant ideology of the Republican Party. The conservative movement has built a network—foundations, think tanks, conservative intellectuals, media outreach—over the last thirty years by meshing philosophical ideas with realpolitik, by which they controlled the debate over issues and took power through governance. Because the Straussians believe in "noble lies," they have no problem using mass deception, as they did when they stressed that weapons of mass destruction (WMD) were the motivating reason for regime change in Iraq. Upon finding no WMDs, the administration then said that was never the sole reason.

Meanwhile, the theoriocracy essentially boxed itself into irrelevance by narrowly focusing on "theoretical" issues regarding power relations in texts, culture, or identity, while neglecting real politics. For example, while the theoriocracy spawned publications like *Social Text* and *Critical Inquiry*, the Right was producing publications like *Public Interest*, *The New Criterion*, *City Journal*, and *The Weekly Standard*, publications that promoted ideas and agendas about power and policies within the public sphere. While Florida Atlantic University began a doctoral program on becoming a "public intellectual," conservative Claremont Graduate School established the Institute for the Study of Statesmanship and Political Philosophy to produce anything but intellectuals. It was interested in producing statesmen, senators, and policymakers, not scholars or academics or intellectuals. Once again, the Right understands its mission: power.

While the Right was steadily entrenching itself in the government and media, the Left would show how incompetent it was by Alan Sokal perpetrating an embarrassing hoax on *Social Text* by submitting a jargon-laden article that purported a link between quantum mechanics and postmodern theory.[23] Instead of understanding the creeping agenda of the Right, the theoriocracy at the University of California at Santa Cruz proposed holding a "workshop" (read: tribunal), not on the conservative movement but on so-called *Left conservatives* (Left/liberals like Sokal or Katha Pollit or Barbara Ehrenreich) who were skeptical about the academy's theory proliferation. Needless to say, the niggarati has aided and abetted this practice and has come up incredibly short and as bankrupt as the rest of the academic Left. That West is an adviser to Al Sharpton is proof-positive. It is also interesting to note that while so-called oppositional public intellectuals have marketed themselves as celebrities, Leo Struass is barely known in the public sphere, but his influence has reached into the top levels of government which control policies that send young men and women out to die.

Anyone with an understanding of what has been going on will come to the bracing realization that the theoriocracy, the academic Left, along with it subset, the niggarati, has been playing a game within its academic warrens for more than a generation. What "old school" conservative intellectuals have been doing, however, is reconstructing the parameters of discourse on public policy issues—as in the case of war—and placing like-minded ideologues within the highest levels of the United States government. Meanwhile, some so-called oppositional public intellectuals with a theoretical bent have suddenly come to the realization that "theory" no longer matters. Maybe, too, intellectuals don't matter in the United States unless they have a decisively rightward thrust.

In short, the whole anti-foundational project of the theoriocracy has collapsed, and most of it was based on the idea that there was no objective truth or facts, just interpretation. Well, as one Dead White Male put it, "Philosophers have only interpreted the world, in various ways; the point is to change it." And the conservatives, for better or for worse, have done that. Can West or Gates ever hope to really inspire a generation of thinkers as in the case of Struass or Edward Said?

Put another way, both the theoriocracy and the niggarati have been, as James Brown once sang, "talkin' loud, but sayin' nothin'."

CHAPTER SIX

THE POLITICS OF ELECTORAL INSTABILITY:
BLACK VOTERS AND STRATEGIC NON-VOTING

And we are sick and tired of hearing your song
Telling how you are gonna change right from wrong
'Cause if you really want to hear our views
You haven't done nothin'!

—Stevie Wonder

After the Republicans routed the Democrats in the 2002 midterm elections, giving the GOP control of both chambers of Congress, a number of postelection postmortems appeared in newspapers and journals throughout the country. In *The Nation*, Ron Walters, a political science professor who teaches at the University of Maryland, wrote a particularly interesting article, "Blacks and the Democratic Party." An explanation of the article's focus said above the title: "Voters Felt Devalued and Heard No Message, So Many of Them Stayed Home." Therein lie the seeds of a potential new relationship between blacks and the Democratic Party, and perhaps with the electoral process.[1]

In the article Walters examined the reasons for the "slight . . . decline" in black voter turnout since 1998. The article appeared when a Republican in a runoff election was challenging Louisiana's Senator Mary Landrieu, a Democrat. Earlier, Landrieu had critically weakened herself by taking her black constituents for granted. Landrieu, however, won the election after receiving a more enthusiastic endorsement from a New Orleans black politician. Blacks, argued Walters, didn't give Democrats a decisive edge in the midterm elections because they heard no one speaking to their concerns about the economy and unemployment. Instead of addressing these issues, the Democrats "wasted . . . political capital by presenting a set of proposals roughly similar to those sought by Bush, including money for tax cuts, protecting state infrastructure from terrorism, the extension of healthcare benefits for the recently employed and school construction."[2]

Interestingly, when speaking of a "real urban policy," Walters accused the Democrats of "abdicating" that for a "less antagonistic focus on schools"—as if education isn't a cornerstone of a real urban policy. Walters's slighting of this concern, while chiding the Democrats, shows how some post-civil rights black intellectuals tend to ignore the salience of education for lower-income blacks, yet are cognizant of the fact that the GOP appears more credible, are "trusted more than Democrats," on education than ever before. This disconnect between black intellectuals and the black rank and file over education is emblematic of how black politics is incapable of addressing an issue of concern to millions of African Americans, namely the education of their children.

Walters also cited how Terry McAuliffe, the Democratic

National Committee chair, initially cold-shouldered Carl McCall's request for more funds as he sought to dislodge Gov. George Pataki as New York's governor. Later, more funds were provided to McCall; however, not enough to save what some thought was already a sputtering campaign. Yet what made the campaign especially ill fated was that Pataki outspent McCall three-to-one. Walters concluded that "unless minority candidates have considerable financial resources of their own to fund their races," black candidates could not depend on the party for assistance. Walters argued how McAuliffe's position ignored "the stunning record of past victories by Democrats that would not have occurred except for the black vote."[3]

Also distressing to Walters was that there were no top black Democratic leaders in the House of Representatives. Democrats haven't had a "black minority or majority leader, caucus chair or whip in the chamber since William Gray in 1991. He further argued that "if black Democratic leaders cannot gain such [leadership] positions, then their ability to transfer their constituents' voting power into public policy is even more severely limited."[4]

Essentially Walters was cataloguing the obvious: the Democratic Party takes the black vote for granted and virtually does everything to hold blacks at arms' length while at the same time being a cosmetically more racially inclusive party than the Republicans. Yet this party crafts "centrist" policies that don't engage blacks but keep them on a tight leash, with black politicians who are more loyal to the party than to their constituents' needs or interests.

Given that Bill Clinton won with an overwhelming black vote and that Al Gore won a large black vote—aided by the NAACP acting as an adjunct by making get-out-the-vote-calls—the Democratic party has a stable and dependable bloc of votes it can go into an election with. Black freelancers like Jesse Jackson, notwithstanding his concern about bringing "issues to the table," have essentially brought more black voters into a relationship of electoral benign neglect without noticeably gaining programs or policies. Al Sharpton, the man who would be Jesse, threatened to do a repeat of the same process.

It is because the black vote has amounted to "appendage politics," as Walters termed it, that the likes of Jackson or Sharpton have risen to engage in HNIC Syndrome politics. This politics is based on the fact that since the black vote is already "locked in," and since blacks have a tendency to become politically disenchanted by the way Democrats take them for granted, cynically posturing, charismatic, black freelancers enter the scene and whip up the black vote during primaries. These spokesmen then parlay their "representing the black community"—a seat at the table—not into "public policy" power but as a means for personal self-aggrandizement as the Indispensable Black Leader. Such leaders are "paid-off" in various ways—travel expenses, one or two inconsequential planks on the party's platform, and usually a rousing speech at the party's convention. And then they go about their business and leave the political stage for the next actor infected with the syndrome. This has been going on for about twenty years, and blacks have become very tolerant of such irresponsible behavior and of anemic representation by duly elected political leaders.

"Blacks should now engage in a serious colloquy," wrote Walters toward the end of the *Nation* article, "to determine an effective strategy for 2004 and beyond, one that does not regard allegiance to the Democratic Party and keeps open other options."[5]

Now is the moment for blacks to consider the merits of creating a new relationship with the Democratic Party and with their political representatives; it is now time for them to consider the merits of *electoral instability*. In other words: *strategic non-voting*.

Blacks should consider strategic non voting as a means to register their displeasure with a political party that needs them as a booster to win elections but jettisons them and their concerns the moment that party obtains the offices it desires. At the beginning of the unofficial campaign season, members of the Democratic Party all entered the race thinking that there is a stable, predictable bloc of votes across the party's political spectrum. What would happen if a certain dependable bloc of voters ignored presidential candidates during crucial primaries?

As well as causing consternation among party elders, such an activity would also delegitimize black political freelancers who essentially use black votes to profit themselves, yet are politically unaccountable. Also, black Democratic politicians who do not fully represent black voters will be put on notice. Pressure will be placed on them to wrangle the black vote back into the Democratic corral.

However, black voters should ask them: What have you done for me lately?

II. THE POLITICS OF ELECTORAL INSTABILITY: STRATEGIC NON-VOTING

What is electoral instability? Electoral instability is when a given party cannot keep its coalition blocs cohesive for the aim of winning elections. African Americans are a bloc of votes for the Democratic Party, and the party is made up of coalitions of voters who adhere to political interests or viewpoints, which are represented by that party. Blacks, according to the 2000 census, make up anywhere from 20 percent to nearly 30 percent of the following Southern states' voting-age populations: Mississippi (33.1), Louisiana (29.7), South Carolina (27.2), Georgia (26.2), Maryland (26.4), Alabama (24), and North Carolina (20). In *key* Electoral College states such as New York (14.8), Florida (12.7), New Jersey (12.6), and Michigan (13.1), mostly Northern states, blacks are roughly 12 percent to 15 percent of those states' voting age populations. By pledging as a *bloc* to withhold their votes from candidates who do not subscribe to their concerns and vigorously pursue them while in office, blacks could begin to exert pressure on the party to move beyond its present role, that of being a sophisticated collection plate.

Black voters, especially Southern blacks since the 1960s and the passage of the Voting Rights Act of 1965, have essentially replaced another set of voters in the Democratic Party, namely conservative white Southerners who left the party to become Republicans. Since the passage of the Voting Rights Act of 1965, blacks—paraphrasing JFK's relationship with being president and reading the newspapers—are voting more but receiving far less for it. As stated above, black voters are an important voting bloc. Their votes allow the Democrats to be competitive when they do mount credible candidates in national and statewide races. However, the black vote is treated as a dependable booster component that rockets white candidates into the orbit of elections, yet black concerns are routinely jettisoned and treated as if they are "special interests." The Democratic Leadership Council's desire for the electorate of choice, meaning white suburban voters, reminds one of a new take on an old Orwellian adage: All voters are equal, but some voters are more equal than others. Politicians, like capital markets, don't like instability. They like predictability and a number of votes they can control and depend on. This is why politicians, notwithstanding the inclusive pablum about bringing in new voters, really don't like extending the franchise beyond a number of votes they are sure of, for it may bring in new voters who are not beholden to them; worse still: a challenger.

Given that the Democratic Party and Republican Party are considered to be the only games worth playing—a "duopoly"—they are made up of coalition elements from Left-liberal-civil rights-labor to Wall Street-Main Street-moderate-religious-conservative axes within the Democratic Party and GOP, respectively. If the United States had a parliamentarian or proportional-representation system, any one of those coalition members might be a party and could run for office representing the interest of those voters who selected them. Instead, the two major parties have forged coalitions around a general set of principles and then set out to win elections from a dwindling electorate while the largest party, the party of non voters, sits out the elections.

However, the aim of strategic non-voting is not based on political *apathy* but to register displeasure with a party that depends on a certain class of voters. Just as any party disciplines wayward politicians either by ousting them, repudiating them, or denying them funds, black voters can do the same. This doesn't mean going over to the GOP; that party has policies that tend not to reflect the concerns of most black voters (despite most black voters being so-called "conservative" on certain social issues). Yet the same can be said of the Democrats. As Micah Sifry, author of *Spoiling for a Fight*, a book on third party politics, observed:

> In the last presidential campaign, Republican George W. Bush and Democrat Al Gore agreed on everything from eliminating the federally guaranteed floor beneath poor mothers (a.k.a. "welfare reform") and increasing the defense budget to expanding the use of the death penalty, deregulating large sectors of the economy, and militarizing the "war on drugs."[6]

What probably makes the Democrats more attractive to blacks than the GOP is that the former still tentatively support positions like affirmative action, and was the party of civil rights. As noted above, however, some of those agreed-upon positions have the tendency to adversely effect lower-income blacks. These are people who tend to be considered expendable by the black political elite and DNC—but who can always be called out as hard-core black Democratic partisans at the lower end of the socioeconomic scale. These are people who may not have much in the way of prestige in their day-to-day existence but may command respect as low-level street functionaries.

In an article on the lone but departing black Republican, Rep. J. C. Watts, which ran in the *Washington Post National Weekly*, a poll by the Joint Center for Political and Economic Studies cited that "63 percent of blacks identified themselves as Democrats, down from 74 percent two years ago."[7] Meanwhile, the number of blacks who identified themselves as Republicans rose from "4 percent to 10 percent."[8] That black identification with Democrats dropped 11 percent in two years points to a nascent electoral instability that could cause Democrats problems. Sifry noted that, generally, from 1990 to 1998, "the proportion of voters registered as independents or third-party has increased approximately 57 percent, while the number of registered Republicans has decreased almost 5 percent and the Democrats almost 14 percent."[9]

Even more interesting, according to the *Washington Post* article, was that Colin Powell scored a higher approval rating "on civil rights" than Jesse Jackson did.[10] That speaks volumes, for it may underscore that Powell, who is not a civil rights leader, is perceived to be something that neither Jackson nor most black Democratic politicians are today, namely an effective political leader who can either solve problems or articulate a vision or a program. (As Bush's secretary of state, however, Powell doesn't appear to have the president's ear on certain policy issues.) One particular problem is the failure of public education.

III. THE FAILURE OF PUBLIC EDUCATION

One of the most critical issues facing blacks is the implosion of the public school system. The Supreme Court's 1954 *Brown v. Board of Education* has been heralded as the decision that sparked the civil rights movement, repudiating the separate but equal doctrine. Yet fifty years later, after court-ordered bussing has been proven a failure, "U.S. Schools Turn More Segregated," according to a *New York Times* article.[11] Seventy percent of black children nationwide, according to a July 2001 study by the Civil Rights Project at Harvard University reported in the *Times* article, attended predominantly segregated minority schools during the 1998–99 school year. Yet effective black leadership has virtually disappeared on this issue; parents have been left to fend for their children's education by considering an option offered by the Republican Party, namely vouchers under the rubric of "school choice." As a matter of fact, noted another *Times* article a year before the previous one:

> While established African American organizations have been among the leaders of the opposition to school vouchers, arguing that they would decimate the public school system, maverick black politicians and community organizers are increasingly the public face of the pro-voucher movement financed largely by white Republican businessmen.[12]

According to a 1999 survey by the Joint Center for Political and Economic Studies, a black-oriented think tank, "60 percent of African Americans favored vouchers" while 53 percent of the overall population does so.[13] However, the pro-voucher support swells to 72 percent among blacks earning less than $15,000. Meanwhile, the center "found that 69 percent of black federal, state, and local elected officials do not support voucher plans," wrote Michael Leo Owens, a political science professor, in an op-ed piece for the *Times*. He continued with an interesting observation:

> Increased black representation in urban public education has had positive *symbolic effects*. There are more black voices in local education policymaking and more black teachers serving as role models. *Nevertheless, the substantive benefits of black electoral representation has been limited*. The educational achievement of black children and the overall quality of urban schools have failed to improve significantly.[14] (Italics added.)

Owens went on to describe the dismal situation regarding education in the pro-black establishment city of Atlanta. He confessed that vouchers had "serious limitations," but understood that for "poor students trapped in the worst schools" it was "enough for black parents to take a chance."[15]

One political reason why black Democratic politicians do not support school vouchers is that the issue affects another member of the Democratic coalition, namely unionized teachers (a potential source of votes and money). There are merits to the arguments that vouchers are an indirect means by which the GOP's is trying to subvert unions. However, neither the national party nor black politicians have credibly addressed the problem of public education for working-class blacks. The GOP's voucher program has the ability to create electoral instability for the Democrats due to the fact that over 70 percent of lower-income blacks, presumably Democratic voters, are for them. And as Sifry has noted, "[I]ndexes of political alienation show that the potential for outside-the-box politics is disproportionately concentrated among people of lower incomes, darker skin, and women."[16]

Meanwhile, the national Democratic Party, the party of most black federal, state, and local elected officials, influenced by the Democratic Leadership Council, desires votes from the electorate of choice, meaning white suburbanites who generally are afforded quality, decent education for their children. However, the GOP, under the present Bush administration, has successfully co-opted the Democrats' position on education. It is considered more trustworthy on that issue than the Democrats.

The Democrats have such a low regard for their most loyal constituents that they would rather have had Trent Lott remain in the position of Senate majority leader. "That would present [the Democratic Party] with a high-profile target to mobilize Democratic voters, particularly blacks, over the next two years," wrote Nagourney and Hulse in the *Times*.[17]

The fact that lower-income blacks would consider the questionable voucher plan proffered by the GOP shows how utterly bereft such a class of African Americans are of effective leadership that would help them solve a pressing problem, the education of their children. That one does not find Jesse Jackson, Rep. Charles Rangel, the NAACP, the Urban League, or so-called black public intellectuals speaking out on such issues speaks volumes about disappearance of effective black leadership, political and intellectual, in the lives of ordinary blacks. Essentially, the national black political directorate that came into being during the 1970s has transformed itself into a compradorian class of agents who, by and large, act more as intermediaries between the white overclass and black constituents. Its supreme goal, it would seem, is to deliver the black vote without disturbing the party's concerns for white swing or independent voters. Its failure is an unacknowledged crisis that can only be resolved by understanding that political change in America is usually based on a crisis.

IV. CRISIS POLITICS

The status of blacks has never changed in American society without an intervening crisis, and there have been at least two. This is due to the fact that the American political system does not readily lend itself to systemic or systematic change. After all, it took the deaths of 700,000 Americans to end slavery, and the economic deprivation of the Great Depression to nominally regulate the economic system to prevent such an occurrence from happening again and allow workers to freely organize for collective bargaining. America is a very dynamic and innovative society. However, given the structure of its politics and political culture, it usually takes a crisis or third-party issues (i.e., the abolition of slavery, child labor laws, women's right to vote, Social Security) to provoke political leaders and ordinary citizens to think beyond politics as usual and institute changes.

In regard to blacks, the Civil War, the first crisis, led to the ending of slavery and changing blacks' status from slaves to citizens. However, state-sanctioned segregation and discrimination kept blacks in second-class citizenship for almost a hundred years after the war, until the civil rights movement, the second crisis, provoked the government into needed political and social reforms in the 1960s. (It should also be noted that the Republican Party, a third party that freed the slaves, abandoned them to their fate in the aftermath of the Compromise of 1877; the deal allowed the Republican Rutherford B. Hayes to become president in exchange for removing federal troops from the South.)

The civil rights movement that was led by King and others during the early years of the 1960s unsettled the Kennedy administration. The bombings, shootings, attacks on freedom rides, marches, whites rioting at the University of Mississippi, and general bad press were an unmitigated public-relations disaster for the United States at the height of the Cold War with the Soviet Union. The New Frontiersmen decided that such activities, namely protesting, if they couldn't be proscribed, could be channeled into political activity such as voter registration.

Both the Kennedy and Johnson administrations, along with civil rights organizations like the Voters Education Project, were able to register voters and get legislation passed that would allow blacks to vote. The Democratic coalition was becoming unstable due to the conflict between the party's Northern black voters and their white allies and its segregationist white Southerners voters. Remember, Lott was waxing exuberantly over Thurmond's bolting the party in 1948, an example of electoral instability for the Democratic Party during the Truman era. Adlai Stevenson's concern for the South in 1952 was the Democratic Party's recognition that the issue of race had to be handled gingerly if the party was to hold on to its Southern base. Yet by the 1960s the Democrats gambled that they would lose the white vote and make up for it by registering black voters.

King and the activists of the civil rights movement were the past masters of engaging in "creative dissent"—Birmingham, Selma, Albany—that forced the government to deal with the status of blacks. However, the powers that be did them one better: they incorporated black disruption of business as usual into the political system. Furthermore, by not having an independent or autonomous political apparatus, the black vote became a dependable adjunct to the Democratic Party. Unlike the civil rights movement, the conservative movement, which learned from the civil rights movement and New Left, established independent organizations—the Moral Majority and the Christian Coalition—as well as burrowing into the GOP.

As the 1960s black freedom movement moved "from protest to politics," community and protest leaders became incorporated into the routines of the country's political system. By the 1970s, some of these leaders became a national black political directorate, with power centered in the Black Congressional Caucus. Meanwhile, black America retired itself from the kind of political action that disrupted business as usual, namely direct action. Political energy was channeled into voting, the only legitimate form of redress of grievances as seen by dominant political elite.

By 1972, close to 1,000 blacks had won elective offices in the South. By the 1976 presidential election, 3.5 million African Americans had been added to voter rolls in the South, and Jimmy Carter won the White House due to the black vote. "The reorganization of the southern wing of the Democratic Party had succeeded," wrote Piven and Cloward *in Poor People's Movements*. "In virtually no time at all the [civil rights] movement had been incorporated into the electoral system, its leaders running for office throughout the South . . ."[18]

However, at this point in time African Americans ought to consider the political advantage of causing electoral instability—in other words, by withholding votes. This would provoke a crisis in the Democratic Party, which needs black votes to win but ignores the issues relating to black voters while chasing after Reagan Democrats and/or the vaunted suburban or swing vote. Blacks should also consider building auxiliary or independent political organizations—not a black party—but groups that would organize the withholding pledges of active voters as a means of political discipline. They would also learn the value of their vote, and that in politics they have neither permanent friends nor permanent enemies, only permanent interests.

V. The Crisis of the National Black Political Directorate

From the late 1960s and 1970s onward, due to the Voting Rights Act of 1965, African Americans increasingly won local, municipal, state, and federal offices in the United States. The most important of these offices were at the federal level, the U.S. Congress. The legislative branch of government formulates public policies and controls allocation of funds and taxation. The formation of the Congressional Black Caucus could be seen as the establishment of a national black political directorate, which represented, at the federal level, the national black community. To a certain degree, the call for "Black Power," interpreted in as many ways by blacks as by whites, had been answered by the rise of the new black political establishment. Its success meant that it had acquired political power at the national level.

However, this success also exposed the new black political elite's very weakness. Robert C. Smith has argued that while the pro-civil rights consensus in Congress has won more than a dozen civil rights or race-specific bills or amendments, "these victories are to an extent irrelevant, symbolic as much as substantive insofar as the life chance of blacks in the United States today." Bills like the Humphrey-Hawkins Full Employment Act in 1978, aimed at chronic black unemployment, wound up being passed as symbolic acts because they were watered down and had no real effect. Interestingly, as Smith noted in Chapter 2, and it bears repeating, the "ghetto constituents" of whom such bills were being aimed were not mobilized.

Black leadership has been fully incorporated not only into the political scheme of things but into the white overclass. It could also be argued that the most important pieces of civil right legislation—the Civil Rights and Voting Rights Acts of the 1960s—had already been passed. Black leadership—political, economic, and intellectual—had boxed blacks into a corner by becoming overly dependent on one method of ameliorating years of political and economic disenfranchisement, through affirmative action and top-down racial management. Unwisely, it had also discarded the kind of political mobilization that led to the dismantling of racial apartheid in the United States and engendered political inclusion. The black elite has never been truly interested in "internal redevelopment" and has often viewed affirmative action programs as a means to that end. What had been a civil rights *movement* had become, in effect, a civil rights *industry*.

Anyone who is remotely aware of the role of today's black politicians cannot help but come to the conclusion that they are essentially irrelevant to their constituents. They haven't been able to mobilize blacks' limited resources to make demands on the larger society, nor have they been able to mobilize blacks for internal redevelopment. During the 1970s, under the Nixon, Ford, and Carter administrations, black leaders were able to get "incremental programmatic benefits," as Aldoph Reed termed them. But that changed when the Republican risorgimento, under Ronald Reagan, rolled into Washington and confronted black leadership and blacks with an unflinching hostility towards civil rights that they were not ready for, much less willing to mobilize against.

Since the 1980s, black political leaders have out-sourced political mobilization to freelance racial spokesmen rather than mobilizing their own constituents. This has led to politics as performance, symbolic political mobilizations like Jackson's 1984 and 1988 presidential runs or Farrakhan's Million Man March. These have occurred at the expense of organizing around issues and programs and monitoring their implementation. This has delegitimized effective black politics. Thus black constituents make less demands on their political leaders and the political system after they realize that so-called leaders like Jackson or Farrakhan are basically pursuing private agendas at the expense of public concerns.

By the 1990s, black politics was so bankrupt that it was not a surprise that large numbers of blacks voted for Bill Clinton. During the 1992 election, Democrats were so desperate to win the White House that Clinton looked, sounded, and smelled like a winner—and he was. The black vote not only has been taken for granted by the Democratic Party, betrayed and ignored by the Republicans since after the Civil War, but has been badly mismanaged by black elected officials who are too timorous to vigorously represent their constituents' interests and fight for them within the political arena. This abdication has led to the development of a pernicious trend in black political culture, the HNIC Syndrome, of which the third installment is represented by the long-tressed, portly countenance of Al Sharpton.

VI. OUTSIDE-THE-BOX POLITICS
How would one go about organizing a voting-bloc boycott of a presidential election? First, one would have to admit that it is going against the grain. The general trend has been to

channel blacks into voting as a means to discourage them from engaging in mass defiance. However, as we have seen in recent years, it is questionable whether or not blacks have their interests represented in matters of the economy, jobs, healthcare, and education, particularly those blacks who are working-class or poor. However, like their white counterparts of the same class status, they have limited influence with the major parities, since they are neither rich nor represent vested economic interest. Also, the social and economic situation of a vast number of African Americans has improved, and the kind of mass defiance that was led by the civil rights movement during the 1960s may no longer be applicable. Instead, rather than confronting the system, blacks may need to *tweak* it.

To tweak the system that would require a sophisticated and daring leadership that understands political calculation and calibration. Unfortunately for blacks, that kind of leadership does not exist today. As already noted, black political leaders, elected and nonelected, have a vested interest in the working of the system as represented by the Democratic Party and, to a lesser degree, the Republican Party. Such black leaders are not willing to lead an electoral revolt. The irony is that the black leadership of the last twenty years, the purported mavericks of the disaffected, HNICers like Jackson and Sharpton, are the very sort of leaders who could possibly lead an electoral revolt of disaffected voters. However, today's mavericks are less interested in challenging the political system; they want, as Richard Nixon characterized it in *his* version of Black Power, "a piece of the action." One only has to recall that the late Ron Brown became chairman of the DNC after being a member of the Jackson campaign, and subsequently oversaw the election of a charter member of the conservative Democratic Leadership Council, Bill Clinton.

Neither individual black leaders nor black organizations have sufficiently reexamined the agenda or tactics of the past three decades of the post-civil rights era. Or perhaps they have and like it the way it is, their protestations notwithstanding. The organizing and synthesizing genius of King, as one political theorist observed, was that he and the movement accomplished in *ten* years, from 1955 to 1965, what the NAACP had not been able to do in *fifty* years of its existence through lobbying and litigation, namely dismantling the legal foundation of segregation. King was able to synthesize Gandhian nonviolence tactics with the redemptive power of suffering and dignity from black religious tradition, as well as borrowing theological ideas and social gospel dollops from leading modern theologians. By being the right individual at the right historical moment, empowered by a community to represent it, King, along with others, was able to forge a social movement. Now is the time, once again, for some creative synthesizing—and organizing.

The best way to harness the use of strategic non-voting, in the view of this chapter, is by way of a new social movement that is generally in formation: black parents who favor school vouchers. What makes them attracted to vouchers is the idea that they can remove their children from bad schools and use vouchers to place them in private or parochial schools, ignoring that such schools are *selective*. However, at the heart of the failure these bad schools, particularly for rural and urban minority communities, is woefully inadequate funding, which is generally derived from states' local property taxes. The lower the property taxes of a given community, the lower the funding for schools in that community's school district. Given how education is the key to social mobility as well as a necessity for functioning in a democratic society based on the notion of self-government, parents who are interested in school vouchers should also demand that *all school districts in the United States have equity in funding.* This would also mean going as far as making up the difference when states are unable; in other words, additional funds from the U.S. Treasury. This, undoubtedly, will be considered controversial due to education having historically been a state and local concern.

However, can a modern nation-state like the United States tolerate an antiquated form of school funding, thus leaving millions of children subjected to a de facto form of racial and class discrimination? Some seem to think so. A New York state judge, in an equity funding case concerning the discrepancy between urban and suburban schools, deemed that the state was only obligated to see that its residents acquired enough of a rudimentary education (up to the 8th grade) to sit on a jury.

Arguably, black parents no longer care if their children are going to integrated schools; the supposition that only by being seated with white children can children of color get a quality education is no longer a major concern. Today, black parents, especially those of lower income, are concerned with the quality of education and would probably embrace an agenda that would make equity of funding for all schools an issue along with an enforcement mechanism to ensure that it happens.

Some figures ought to be kept in mind: 60 percent of African Americans favor vouchers, and 63 percent of blacks identify themselves as Democrats, a decline from 74 percent. Also, almost 70 percent of black federal, state, and local elected officials do not support voucher plans, and one can favorably conjecture that these officials' children probably attend either private schools or the better public schools in cities and suburbs. Black support for vouchers rises to 72 percent for those whose income is less than $15,000. There is a social gap between black representatives and the realities that face their constituents, as well a social base to organize a potential movement of parents who feel that their children are being mis educated.

This educational movement would be, in fact, a social movement initially made up of a social stratum of parents who do vote and whose children are at risk of being mis-educated by inadequately funded public education systems throughout the country. This movement would also seek to enter into coalitions with other educational reform organizations, but it should also press the equity-in-funding issue to state and federal Democratic officials or to those who seek to replace them in elections.

Now is the time for blacks to engage in a form of domestic realpolitik, with the understanding that the Democratic Party is less interested in pursuing a "progressive" agenda and more interested in merely winning elections. While some black leaders invoke the progressive legacies of Roosevelt, Kennedy, and Johnson, they often ignore the rank political calculations, wheeling and dealing, and arm-twisting these presidents made in order to get legislation passed. Blacks, who make up a significant voting bloc as other Americans vote less, ought to pursue tactics and strategies that enhance their interests. One way to do this is to provide a *negative* sanction against the party that has made triangulation at their expense a fine political art. Blacks could in engage in a pincer attack on the Democrats. With the GOP offering vouchers and President Bush's "No Child Left Behind" education act passed, an organized movement by educationally disenfranchised blacks should demand a program for universal equity in school funding.

Once again, strategic non-voting is not for the apathetic. Its aim is to make the vote of black Americans, and all Americans, more meaningful than it is in the current atmosphere of corrosive civic disengagement. To make a case for not voting goes against the grain of what blacks have achieved in the last thirty-five years or so. Electoral instability is also fraught with risks. Some in the Democratic Party would be happy if the image of the party wasn't too identified with black concerns. Perhaps sitting out an election, making the party not look "too black," may be what some in the party actually want. Even if this is true, the Democrats would crumble if the black vote were not in the electoral mix. The 2000 election was extremely close, and most of the votes disqualified in Florida were—surprise!—black votes, which Al Gore didn't too energetically defend as a civil rights or voting rights issue. Once again, the black vote is needed by the party but is also taken for granted by it. The NAACP made a considerable effort to get black voters to the polls, almost crossing the line into partisan politics. Yet it says virtually nothing about the implosion of public education, nor does it offer solutions. Non-voting is not a tactic that is to be applied every time; it needs to be applied judiciously and under the right circumstances.

However, one has to question the sanctity of the vote, the actual worth of the vote. If by casting it—investing political power in others—those who do vote receive so little in the way of programs and/or policies, then their life chances in a democratic society are negligible. Racial profiling, police brutality, unemployment, inadequate housing, healthcare, and substandard education buffet a third of African Americans. Yet the Democratic Party, dominated if not controlled by the DLC, expects black Democratic partisans to "energize" their most loyal base. At some point, African Americans have to assume some responsibility for their relationship with Democrats. Even the man who would be Jesse, Al Sharpton, asserts that blacks are themselves at fault for not holding the Democrats' feet to the fire.

"I don't blame the candidates; I blame that on us," said Sharpton in an interview. "We need to stop allowing our communities to be photo ops for Democrats who won't address our issues. For a party that gets 92 percent of our vote, I mean, this is ridiculous. They should be dealing with these issues across the board."[19]

True, but African Americans ought to stop letting individuals like Sharpton stand in for them as leaders when he

and others represent a bankrupt, corrupt, and antidemoc-
ratic form of political representation that is based more on
egocentric brokerage than engaged mass empowerment.

Given what blacks actually get out of the political system
and from their so-called leaders, perhaps strategic non-voting
may be well worth considering.

Postscript
Scampaign 2004

"The only reason he's running is either he's an egomaniac or as a Bush contract. What's the point? This is not 2000 when progressives were locked out. I'm going on a national crusade to stop Nader. This is only going to help Bush."

Thus spoke Al Sharpton commenting on the either crazed or corrupt Ralph Nader who had decided to become a presidential contender in 2004 election. What was eerie about Sharpton's response was the bombastic self-righteousness and condemnation of Nader: he was muscling in on Sharpton's "progressive" mandate, as if there can only be one or two in the race. The unreal aspect to Sharpton's response, however, was that it was said in the aftermath of the fact that it had been revealed that he himself was, so to speak, a "Bush contract."

Rather than using the Internet as a means to solicit money and build an organization as Howard Dean did, Sharpton, instead, began an association with the devil himself in the form of the Republican Party. Wayne Barrett, a reporter for *The Village Voice*, documented such a relationship between Sharpton, supposedly a Democrat, and Roger Stone, a Republican "dirty-tricks operative" who "led the mob that shut down the Miami-Dade county recount and helped make

George W. Bush president in 2000." According to Barrett's detailed article ("Sleeping with the GOP," February 4-10, 2004), Stone was "financing, staffing, and orchestrating" Sharpton's presidential campaign.

When confronted with this peculiar relationship and how it contradicted his campaign that was supposedly against Bush's party and policies, Sharpton replied that the *Voice*'s inquiries were standard "phony liberal paternalism." Sharpton, however, admitted to talking to Stone but denied him being an adviser. When Frank Watkins, Jesse Jackson's previous campaign manager, left Sharpton's campaign, in stepped Charles Halloran, an associate of Stone who has worked on previous Democratic campaigns but is essentially a hired-gun in association with Stone. As a matter of fact, in a subsequent *Voice* article ("Sharpton's Cynical Campaign Choice," February 11-17, 2004), it was revealed that Sharpton was using Watkins as a walking Potemkin Village while talking to Stone and turning over power to Halloran.

However, more interesting is that in order for Sharpton to win matching funds under the Federal Election Commission's guidelines, which stipulates that a campaign must draw threshold funds of $100,000 from twenty states, Stone, a Republican, admitted to collecting checks on Sharpton's behalf to meet that criteria. "Sharpton," wrote Barrett, "was the last candidate to meet the December 31 [2003] deadline and is immediately seeking more than $150,000 in federal funding." The *New York Times* had spotlighted issues regarding Sharpton's financial operations and his association with Roger Stone before. However, those issues were merely tips of

the proverbial iceberg in regard to Sharpton's extensive relationship with a GOP operative that assisted in the scheme to
disenfranchise black voters.

Despite the connivance and corruption, Cornel West
argued that Sharpton provided a service. "I'm glad Sharpton's
there because he kept the [the Democrats] honest. They been
so spineless when it comes to the legacy of white supremacy,"
he said in another *Voice* article ("Running from Race," February 11-17, 2004). Of course, black America's greatest mind
would never address the issue of keeping those who purport
to be black leaders honest. Nor would he dare suggest that
blacks begin some real organizational efforts on their own
rather than trying to convince whites to live up their legacy.
That wouldn't make him popular or critical. Neither did one
hear a round of denunciation from black established black
leadership about Sharpton's corruption.

Sharpton's presidential bid, however, was essentially a
scampaign to supplant Jackson as the next HNIC. In order to
do so he solicited votes from black churches, tried to elicit
money from taxpayers via the FEC, and became dependent
upon expertise and money from the very same people who
have participated in black disenfranchisement. Sharpton
knew he used the likes of West, Michael Eric Dyson, and
others to provide ideological cover for his corrupt maneuver-
ings. In essence, Sharpton had no real vision or organization
to propel an agenda that was supposedly about grassroots
mobilization, and his dependence on Stone and poor showing
in the South Carolina primary underscored that.

In the South Carolina Democratic primary, for example,

he was bested by two white candidates, Senators John Edwards and John Kerry, of North Carolina and Massachusetts, respectively. He only won 19 percent of the black vote while Edwards won 36 percent and Kerry won 32 percent. Overall, he placed a distant third behind Edwards and Kerry who won 45 and 30 percent of the votes in South Carolina. Sharpton had only won a measly 10 percent. His game plan was to pick up delegates as a means to use them as leverage at the Democratic convention; he didn't win any in South Carolina.

Sharpton's political opportunism made him an attractive target for GOP dirty tricksters. He offers the possibility of being an "independent" candidate to run against Hillary Clinton in 2006, reported Barrett. True to the Massa complex within the HNIC Syndrome, Sharpton's desire to teach white liberals a lesson and make them respect him, allowed the GOP to use him for their own purposes, which is basically to cause mischief in Democratic politics by keeping him in the game. In so many ways Sharpton's behavior and resentment politics recalls the Darth Vader of American politics, Richard Nixon. They both have the same thuggish mien and use politics basically as a means to an end, not one of advancing goals and agenda but settling scores. Better still, Sharpton is basically a black version of Richard Nixon with all the same self-destructive tendencies. Perhaps, we Americans are now truly equal.

Implicit in this critique of the HNIC syndrome, in which Sharpton is the third installation, is that it tends to be male dominated, which has led to a dead-end in regard to black politics. One of the results of the black liberation struggles of

the late 1960s and 1970s, and even in the civil rights movement of the mid-1950s and early 1960s, was the machismo
that led to the shunting aside of capable black women into
auxiliary roles. This was despite women having a record—a
history!—of organizational and leadership capabilities.
Women such as Septima Clark, Ella Baker, Cynthia Washington, Fannie Lou Hamer, Gloria Richardson and countless
others were never given their due as organizers and as leaders.

Nothing was more obnoxious than the idea that "sisters
should stay home and have babies for the revolution" and
"support the warrior brothers" during the so-called black liberation phase. This mindset, one of the original examples of
black orthodoxy, often led to a cult of the gun over figuring
out an effective politics truly based on people's genuine
needs. One could even see a version of this machismo in
mainstream black politics when Rep. Shirley Chisholm
(D-NY) was nominated in 1972; she suffered the ire of black
men who resented that a black woman had even been considered over them! Not one of the leading black organizations
of the civil rights period—SCLC, NAACP, SNCC, CORE—
was ever led by a black woman despite the fact that women
were getting bitten by dogs, jailed, beaten, and murdered
during that period.

Within the last year publications such as *Newsweek*, *The
American Prospect* and *Atlantic Monthly* have run articles about the
so-called "black gender gap." Often noted is the fact that
black women seem to be doing better than black men in education and work. No one, however, has significantly,
addressed the black women leadership gap—not even

Michael Eric Dyson who speaks of his love for black women. Black women are sorely needed as political leaders because black men have sorely botched any effective black politics in the last twenty years.

Just as we have argued that one of the crucial mistakes of black politics has been going from protest to politics without an independent political base, putting aside creative disruption for anemic incorporation, even more damaging to African American political culture has been the turning of black women into virtual nonentities in the political world. One also should wonder if black women are doing well in education and work, which are normally used as criteria for political office consideration, why aren't they acceding to positions of leadership? It's as if one has loped off half of one's brain and wonders why one can't think.

Towards the end of King's momentous 1963 speech, he announced that he was returning to the South with a faith that "will be able to hew out of the mountain of despair a stone of hope." Thirty-six years after his assassination that stone of hope has now become a huge boulder named Al Sharpton, tied around the neck of black America as it sinks deeper into the dark gloomy waters of black orthodoxy. This will be the legacy of Scampaign 2004.

APPENDIX
PRESIDENT'S URBAN STRATEGY
(CISNEROS MEMO)

If one wants to get a good idea of a missed opportunity during the Clinton years, one only need to read the following memo from then–Secretary of Housing and Urban Development Henry Cisneros. Some aspects of the "President's Urban Strategy" were adopted, including enterprise zones that offered—as usual—tax breaks for businesses if they planted themselves in blighted neighborhoods. Pay special attention to the ideas regarding "empowerment schools," "fresh start academies" and converting "public housing complexes to campuses for learners," or to "electronic villages." These are the seeds of a possible return to the kind of agenda and organizing that the pre–Black Power SNCC engaged in, namely raising up indigenous local leadership and helping everyday people figure out what they want to do and how to go about doing it. For a history of that lost agenda read Clayborne Carson's *In Struggle* and John Dittmer's *Local People*.

U.S. DEPARTMENT OF HOUSING AND URBAN DEVELOPMENT

THE SECRETARY

WASHINGTON, D.C. 20410-8001
August 9, 1995

MEMORANDUM FOR: President Bill Clinton
FROM: Henry C. Cisneros
SUBJECT: President's Urban Strategy

At our first Cabinet meeting, you said that if Cabinet Officers ever had an urgent message which we felt you should see that we should put it in a memo and you would review it. Knowing of the immense demands on your attentions I have tried not to abuse that privilege, but I want now to convey to you in the strongest terms that the time is now or never for a Presidential urban strategy.

I am not making a self-serving plea for budget or programs; this is not a call for a HUD urban strategy. I believe it is time for a Presidential strategy which either takes the form of a definable White House effort or which combines the urban initiatives of several Departments in a cohesive way. I am acutely aware of budget and Congressional barriers, but there are overarching reasons why a Presidential initiative is urgent:

1. *The cities are hurting badly and the nation will pay the consequences for many years:*

The effects of the Congressional budget cuts further erode urban conditions that were already dangerously deteriorated. Economic vitality and jobs have been zapped from city after city. Daily we lose more of our inner city children to drugs, gangs, and guns. We must draw deeply on our experience and determine the two or three most important things that can make a difference. I have outlined some suggestions herein.

2. *We are running out of time:*

The 1997 budget you will prepare this fall is the last one this term in which you can offer a credible urban package.

3. *There is always room in the budget for Presidential Priorities of reasonable size:*

If you decide early in the budget process that an urban program is needed, it will be a factor throughout the entire budget process instead of an afterthought that cannot be accommodated because it would push out other spending late in the game.

4. *We do not have enough to stand on in the cities:*

Empowerment zones [EZ] in 12 cities are simply not a broad enough program to stand on. We have to have something cooking that is more broadly based and hopeful to more cities.

5. *We can be caught flat-footed by the violent outbreaks which will stem from the anger in the cities:*

There have been three contained outbreaks of civil unrest in recent weeks—Indianapolis, Coconut Grove outside Miami, and Los Angeles (see attached descriptions and a column from the *Boston Globe*).* Many local leaders are worried that it won't take much to set off wider disturbances. We do not want to be caught flat-footed if civil unrest occurs, which increasing numbers of local leaders feel is inevitable.

Mr. President, for all of these reasons I recommend that you consider one or a combination of the following kinds of urban initiatives as a centerpiece of the 1997 budget, with an announcement as soon as possible that you intend to do it.

The central theme of these suggestions is that they expand economic opportunities for residents of distressed communities and put people to work:

A. Building Competitive Cities: Connecting People to Work

1. *Draw Private investment to the cities by lowering the business tax burden:*

The challenge is to get the capital markets to respond to the cities. A commercial revitalization tax credit for distressed communities would replicate the success of the low-income housing tax credits. The credits could spur private investments

*not included. −author.

to generate jobs as well as provide needed community amenities, such as neighborhood shopping districts.

One approach would be to pursue a second round of empowerment zones matched to tax strategies, such as:

—capital gains relief to businesses that reinvest gains in an EZ business asset;
—a portable tax credit, allowing businesses outside the zones credit for hiring residents who live in these communities; and
—a welfare-to-work credit for businesses who hire EZ residents who currently receive AFDC benefits.

The Vice President's involved leadership on the first round of zones has spurred an unprecedented level of community organization and strategic planning. The zones are proving their ability to leverage substantial private capital (Lead Agency: Treasury)

2. *Prime the pump with smart public investment:*
The most flexible and successful tools available to local officials for local economic development are HUD's Section 108 and Economic Development Initiative. In FY 1995 alone, the combination of these two programs has helped 70 communities create or retain over 70,000 jobs. The assistance has leveraged billions in public and private investment and has supported such key efforts as the creation of small business revolving funds and the location of inner-city

supermarkets. The Mayors describe it as the most effective federal money to use for local economic development, though Commerce's EDA funds are also very effective.

The House Appropriations Bill drastically curtails these programs, reducing the limitation on Section 108 loan guarantees from $2.05 billion to $1 billion and eliminating the $350 million Economic Development Initiative completely. These were the kinds of funds used to make possible the Los Angeles CD bank. A wide variety of local job generation strategies can be built on expansion of these programs. (Lead Agencies: HUD and Commerce)

OR

3. *Spur Community Development Banks modeled on the Los Angeles Community Development Bank:*

This initiative deals with a critical linkage connecting people to work—increasing access to job creating debt capital in the inner city through the creation of CD banks. It builds upon a successful model pioneered in Los Angeles by Mayor Riordan. Vice President Gore has called the Los Angeles community development bank "a model of innovation and creativity for the rest of the nation." If the CDFI appropriation remains mired (it was reduced to $50 million as a result of the FY 1995 recissions bill and receives no funding in the FY 1996 appropriations bill) it should be remembered that the Los Angeles bank was the result of HUD's Economic Development Initiative and

Section 108 programs. They can be a vehicle for putting some banks in place now. (Lead Agency: Treasury and HUD)

OR

4. *Reclaim environmentally unsafe central city land and provide training and jobs in clean-up and redevelopment*:

One of the most challenging problems facing cities is the clean-up and clearance of old industrial sites that in their existing condition are barriers to redevelopment. Contaminated land represents more that 40 percent of Cleveland, more than 20 square miles of Philadelphia, and thousands of acres of Detroit.

Cities need land that is cleared and free of environmental hazards before they can begin to make businesses or housing strategies work. Capital grants to clean-up "brownfields" can be matched to training funds to employ central city residents in environmental clean-up activities. Available land and ready capital will form a powerful combination to help cities exploit their competitive economic advantages and attract back middle-income homeowners. The scale of this effort should be to clear sites of hundreds of acres so that large scale business developments and subdivisions of up to a thousand homes for homeownership can be built. (Lead Agencies: EPA and Labor)

OR

5. *Expand the Bridges—to—Work Demonstration to a National Scale*:

"As I try to show in my own work, decades of poverty concentration and job suburbinization have isolated the poor residents of many inner cities from the areas of greatest employment opportunity in their metropolitan regions. While efforts to reduce poverty concentration and so reverse job suburbanization remain important national priorities (e.g. fair housing enforcement and empowerment zones, respectively), Bridges—to—Work would test a third and complementary approach: directly connecting inner city residents to job opportunities outside their local communities." (William Julius Wilson, in letter to Secretary Cisneros, June 15, 1995.)

The Bridges-to-Work demonstration (BtW) is an exciting initiative that directly connects inner-city residents to job opportunities outside their local communities. Five national foundations (Ford, Rockefeller, MacArthur, Casey, and Pew) are supporting Public/Private Ventures (PP/V) to design this eight-site national demonstration. During the course of two years of intensive development work, PP/V has assembled an impressive set of eight potential sites including metropolitan Chicago, Philadelphia, St. Louis, Baltimore, Denver, Milwaukee, St. Paul, and Newark. These eight partner sites have formed planning collaboratives representing interests from throughout their regions and have developed detailed Bridges—to—Work projects that are ready to be implemented. William Julius Wilson called Bridges—to—Work the "single most important anti-poverty R+D initiative underway in the

Administration." FY 1997 is the time to expand Bridges–to–Work to a national scale by providing modest federal planning grants to metropolitan planning collaboratives across the country, enabling them to replicate the accomplishments of the demonstration sites. (Lead Agency: Labor)

B. Express our Commitment to our Children and Youth

1. *Create a Network of "Empowerment Schools" and "Fresh Start Academies":*

Despite all our current efforts, we stand in jeopardy of losing a large proportion of inner-city youth to the streets. The statistics are grim and unrelenting. Drop-out rates in inner-city high schools typically approach 50 percent. One-half of all African–American male school dropouts under the age 25 are now under criminal justice supervision. The employment rate of such dropouts is less than 40 percent.

If any urban strategy is to be successful, we need to address these problems head-on, building upon the lessons of the efforts to date. Two ideas have emerged which, I believe, hold great promise.

The first is to create a network of "empowerment schools" that would stimulate community-wide collaborations and comprehensive strategies for supporting parents, children, and youth. As in the successful empowerment zones, communities (including private business) would be challenged to offer integrated solutions that cross agencies and disciplines.

Communities would be given the latitude and flexibility to combine existing programs as well as compete for new funding. The possibilities for marrying what are now disparate and unconnected federal funding streams—public housing, Head Start, school-to-work, summer jobs—are endless.

The second idea, which is complementary, is to offer a fresh start to troubled youth by providing them with disciplined, structured environments. One approach is to support a network of "Fresh Start Academies" that could offer four years of quality education and vocational training in an environment of character-building discipline. Graduates would be guaranteed college scholarships. There is great potential for the use of retired military personnel in such an effort. (Lead Agency: Education)

C. Linking the Cities to the Momentum of the Information Age

1. *Convert public housing complexes to campuses for learners:*

Public housing complexes can be restructured as learning campuses, as universities for the residents, as homes to communities of learners. The housing units become dormitories which support the classrooms and computer rooms nearby for residents of all ages—developmental day care for children, public schools adjacent to the campus for the youth, training and college curricula for adults, and self-improvement classes for seniors. Classes are held every day on-campus, given by faculty who commute there or live there.

Every residential apartment can be wired to offer the computer connections necessary to make self-paced learning possible at all hours. The information highway need not bypass distressed neighborhoods or poor people.

The psychological difference between public housing as it is and this concept of communities of learners is that, like at a university, residents at the "learning campus" are not viewed as permanent but for as long as the educational process takes. The ever-present expectation is self-improvement and the quest for eventual self-sufficiency. For all but seniors, residential tenure is limited to no more than four years, consistent with the duration of the curriculum. (Lead Agency: HUD)

OR

2. *Seed inner cities with a network of "electronic villages"*:

In the same way that the interstate highway system bypassed poor and disadvantaged communities, accelerating their economic and social decline, the information superhighway could bypass and further isolate distressed communities and their residents from the social and economic mainstream.

The theory behind this initiative is that by providing residents of lower income neighborhoods with the primary tools of access to today's information economy, barriers will fall and positive economic results will begin to accrue. This initiative would help fund a network of learning-oriented inner-city neighborhood centers which connect residents, businesses, service providers, and government in a community network. It would build upon and expand FHA's current initiative in the Edgewood community in NE Washington, and upon efforts to train residents in computer literacy and create resident-owned businesses based upon computer technology. Tremendous economic gains would result, for example, by amending CRA to give leaders CRA credit for subcontracting a small fraction of their back-office data-processing operations to resident-owned firms.

Pushing the envelope on electronic villages and the broader concept of electronic community development would require the close coordination of HUD, Commerce, Education, and Labor—each of which is experimenting with how to bring the benefits of 21st century technology to inner cities. This initiative builds on the Vice President's interests in the information super highway and is a win-win initiative for all concerned. (Lead Agencies: Labor, Education, Commerce, HUD)

CONCLUSION

Mr. President, it is obvious that government alone cannot solve the problem of the cities. We will change the course of inner-city life only if the nation commits both private and public energies, talent, and resources. Churches, family, involved adults, volunteerism, boys and girls clubs—these are the real means for reweaving the social fabric in our distressed communities.

This issue offers you an opportunity to have a sober conversation with the nation on the American future and potential. It places you in a position above party and above individual gain. You are at your best—national service, the Memphis speech, the Affirmative Action decisions—when you lift the national dialogue to a higher, even spiritual, level where you encourage and exhort individuals and communities to fulfill a higher purpose.

Again, I am not advocating for any one of these proposals individually so much as making the case that you and the nation need an urban message. I would like to back-up this case with the opportunity to speak with you and expand upon the urgency of the nation's urban condition.

Ten Things That Could Be Done to Revitalize Black Politics

1. Recognize that black politics has regressed and has been demobilized, and that greater organizational and institutional effort has to be emphasized, not symbolic posturing.

2. Return to the original intent of the Rainbow Coalition for black politics: develop an agenda driven, grassroots, voter mobilization politics.

3. Refer to the Cisneros Memo (President's Urban Agenda) as a model for an urban agenda as well as thinking about a rural agenda for rural-based blacks.

4. Develop a national caucus-based politics in localities that demands news ideas, methods, and action from local and national black political leaders and black intellectuals; caucuses should consider running grassroots candidates for local offices based on accountability, communication and transparency (ACT).

5. Develop black think tanks that will look critically at problems and issues affecting blacks and create plans and policies to assist organizations that are addressing issues and problems.

6. Black economic development should be based on a "new institutionalism" that is an intelligent blend of private capital, community-owned, cooperatively run, and state-supported enterprises.

7. An effective public affairs communication infrastructure needs to be developed—radio, television, magazines, journals, internet, books, etc.—that critically looks at issues in the realm of politics, culture, economics, and gender relations.

8. Encourage black women to seek a larger leadership role in black politics since they are often the primary caregivers and are affected by public/social policies decisions in regard to work, education, taxation, etc.

9. The black church, the fount of black political culture, needs to become more actively engaged in attending to its congregation's and black America's temporal needs. Jesus, according to the Bible, attended to people's temporal and spiritual needs.

10. Rather than concentrating on slavery reparations, lawyers, historians, economists and activists ought to scrutinize the relationship between blacks and the music recording industry, which has often been one of rank exploitation. Why is it that blacks have developed various genres of music yet have no significant control over an industry that is based on their talent?

NOTES

INTRODUCTION

1 Neil Postman, *Amusing Ourselves to Death: Public Discourse in the Age of Show Business* (New York: Penguin Books, 1985) pp. 3-4.

2. And this branding has made him a relatively wealthy man compared to most academics, earning him nearly $ 2 million per year from speaking engagements, while also cranking out rap CDs, appearing in films, and offering intellectually anemic work.

2. Cornel West, *Prophesy Deliverance!: Afro-American Revolutionary Christianity* (Philadelphia: The Westminster Press, 1982), p. 50.

3. Genesis 9:20 – 25.

4. Colossians 3:22

5. Colossians 4:1

6. West, *Prophesy Deliverance!*, p.16.

7. E. Franklin Frazier, *Black Bourgeoisie* (New York: Macmillan Publishing Co., 1957), p. 112.

8. Eugene D. Genovese, *Roll Jordan, Roll: The World the Slaves Made* (New York: Random House, 1976), p. 6; See also Part 1 "Of the Living God," pp. 161–284.

9.Allison Calhoun-Brown, "Will the Circle Be Unbroken?", Johnson and Stanford, eds., *Black Political Organizations in the Post-Civil Rights Era* (New Brunswick: Rutgers University Press, 2002), p. 25.

10. For a history of American anti-intellectualism, see Richard Hofstader's *Anti-intellectualism in American Life* (New York: Vintage, 1963); see also Henry Steele Commager's "Leadership in Eighteenth-Century America and Today" (*Daedalus*, 90 1961). That period was probably the last time American society was actually led by intellectuals.

11. Katharine Q. Seelye, "Black Leaders Give Clinton Forgiveness and Support," *New York Times*, September 21, 1998.

12. Dan T. Carter, *The Politics of Rage: George Wallace, the Origins of the New Conservatism, and the Transformation of American Politics* (New York: Simon & Schuster, 1995), p. 74.

13. David J. Garrow, *Bearing the Cross: Martin Luther King, Jr. and the Southern Christian Leadership Conference* (London: Vintage, 1986), pp. 584-586.

14. Stanley Crouch, "Rev. Al is Going for a Lot More Than Glory," *New York Daily News*, Dec. 18, 2003, p. 47.

CHAPTER ONE: THE HEAD NEGRO IN CHARGE SYNDROME AND THE MAN WHO WOULD BE JESSE

1. W. E. B. Du Bois, *The Souls of Black Folk* (New York: Gramercy Books, 1994), p. 146.

2. *Brian Lehrer Show*, WNYC (audio file), www.wnyc.org/shows/bl/episodes/12112003.

3. H.H. Gerth and C. Wright Mills, eds., *From Max Weber: Essays in Sociology* (New York: Oxford University Press, 1972), p. 246.

4. Cornel West, *Prophesy Deliverance!: Afro-American Revolutionary Christianity* (Philadelphia: The Westminster Press, 1982). p. 36.

5. Witness both Rice's and Powell's participation in the Bush administration's deceptive rationalization for the war in Iraq in *The Five Biggest Lies Bush Told Us About Iraq*.

6. *Parting the Waters; Pillar of Fire*

7. *A Question of Character*

8. Alan Feur; "An Open Message for Bill Clinton: Your Neighbors in Harlem Miss You Like Crazy." *The New York Times*, Nov. 17, 2003.

9. Stanley Crouch, "Rev. Al is Going for a Lot More Than Glory," *New York Daily News*, Dec. 18, 2003, p.47.

10. Associated Press, www.msnbc.com/news/854722.asp?0cv=CB10, January 3, 2003.

11. Todd Gitlin, *The Whole World Is Watching: Mass Media in the Making and Unmaking of the New Left* (Berkeley: University of California Press, 1980), p. 147

12. Ibid., p. 152.

13. Ibid., p. 166.

14. Attributed to former DC mayor Marion Barry in regard to Jesse Jackson.

15. Martin Kilson, "The Weakness of Black Politics," *Dissent*, Fall 1987, pp. 523–529.

16. Citation #16: Jerry GafioWatts, *Amiri Baraka: The Politics and Art of a Black Intellectual* (New York: New York University Press, 2001), pp. 476-477.

CHAPTER TWO: FOLLOW THE LEADERS?

1. Jerry Gafio Watts, *Amiri Baraka: The Politics and Art of a Black Intellectual* (New York: New York University Press, 2001), pp. 314-315.

2. Robert Novak, "How Farrakhan could energize the Republicans," *The New York Post*, March 6, 1997, p. 31.

3. Adolph Reed, *Class Notes* (New York: The New Press, 2000), p.61

4. Claude A. Clegg III, "You're Not Ready for Farrakhan," *Black Political Organizations in the Post-Civil Rights Era*, Ollie Johnson III and Karin L. Sanford , eds. (New Brunswick: Rutgers University Press, 2002), p. 131.

5. Robert C. Smith, *We Have No Leaders* (Albany, State University of New York Press, 1996), pp. 10-11.

6. Bayard Rustin, "From Protest to Politics: The Future of the Civil Rights Movement," *Down the Line* (Chicago: Quadrangle Books, 1971), p.119.

7. See Rustin's memo to King, "Memo on the Spring Protest in Washington, D.C." re the Poor People's Campaign in *Down the Line: The Collected Writings of Bayard Rustin*, pp. 202–5.

8. Smith, *We Have No Leaders*, p. 183.

9. Smith, *We Have No Leaders*, p. 210.

10. Michael Lind, *The Next American Nation* (New York: Free Press, 1995), p.162.

11. Alexander Cockburn, "The Book of Numbers," *New York Press*, January 21-27, p.11.

12. Ron Walters, "Blacks and the Democratic Party," *The Nation*, December 16, 2002.

13. Adam Nagourney and Carl Hulse, "Bush Rebukes Lott Over Remarks on Thurmond," *New York Times*, December 13, 2002, p. A36.

14. For an excoriating review of Steele's book, see Adolph Reed's review, "Steele Trap," *The Nation*, March 4, 1991, pp. 274-281.

15. Ronald V. Walters and Robert C. Smith, *African American Leadership* (Albany: State University of New York Press, 1999), p. 82.

16. Sally Covington, "Moving A Public Policy Agenda: The Strategic Philanthropy of Conservative Foundations" (Washington, DC: National Committee for Responsive Philanthropy, 1997); Jean Stefancic and Richard Delagado, *No Mercy: How Conservative Think Tanks and Foundations Changed America's Social Agenda* (Philadelphia: Temple University Press, 1998); Sidney Blumenthal, *The Rise of a Counter-Establishment: From Conservative Ideology to Political Power* (New York: Times Books, 1986); Deborah Toler, "Black Conservatives, "The Public Eye" (Somerville: Political Research Associates, 1993). Nina J. Easton, *Gang of Five: Leaders at the Center of the Conservative Ascendancy* (New York: Touchstone, 2000). Joseph Conti, Brad Stetson, *Challenging the Civil Rights Establishment: Profiles of a New Black Vanguard* (Westport: Praeger, 1993). Angela D. Dillard, *Guess Who's Coming to Dinner Now?: Multicultural Conservatism in America* (New York: New York University Press, 2001).

17. Smith, *We Have No Leaders*, p. 135.

18. See Adam Shatz's article on Loury's "rehabilitation" in the *New York Times Magazine*, "Glenn Loury's About Face," January 20, 2002.

19. James E. Clingman, "Turning 'Spending Weakness' Into Power," www.sacobserver.com/business/commentary/091603/black_spending_we akness.shtml.

20. David J.Garrow, *Bearing the Cross: Martin Luther King, Jr. and the Southern Christian Leadership Conference* (London: Vintage, 1986), p. 266.

21. Frances Fox Piven and Richard A. Cloward, *Poor People's Movements: How They Succeed, How They Fail* (New York: Vintage, 1979), p. 254.

22. W. E. B. Du Bois, *Dusk of Dawn: An Essay Toward an Autobiography of Race* (News Brunswick: Transaction Publishers, 1995). p. 198.

23. Harold Cruse, *The Crisis of the Negro Intellectual* (New York: Quill, 1984), p. 314.

24. Cruse, *The Crisis of the Negro Intellectual*, p. 328.

CHAPTER 3: THE ROOTS OF SYMBOLIC POLITICS

1. Benjamin Muse, *The American Negro Revolution: From Nonviolence to Black Power* (New York: Citadel Press, 1970) p.236

2. David J. Garrow, *Bearing the Cross: Martin Luther King and the Southern Christian Leadership Conference* (London: Vintage Books, 1993), p. 477.

3. Ibid. In re to tensions between SCLC and NAACP, see pp. 71-72,78, 91-92, 134, and 166; SCLC and SNCC, 404-6, 409-10, 414, 423-424, 440-41. Also see Taylor Branch's *Parting the Waters* and *Pillar of Fire*.

4. Charles V. Hamilton, *Adam Clayton Powell: The Political Biography of an American Dilemma* (New York: Atheneum, 1991), p. 336. See also *Bearing the Cross*, pp. 139-40.

5. *Bearing the Cross*, p. 485.

6. Ibid., p. 481.

7. Ibid., p. 485. See also Martin Luther King's *Where Do We Go From Here: Chaos or Community?* (Boston: Beacon, 1967), pp. 29-31.

8. *Bearing the Cross*, p. 436.

9. Claude Andrew Clegg, *An Original Man: The Life and Times of Elijah Muhammad* (New York: St. Martin's Press, 1997) p. 157

10. Ibid., p. 163.

11. Ibid., p 115.

12. Ibid., pp. 115-6.

13. Ibid., p. 116.

14. William W. Sales, Jr. *From Civil Rights to Black Liberation: Malcolm X and Organization of Afro-American Unity* (Boston: South End Press) p. 46.

15. Rod Bush, *We Are Not What We Seem: Black Nationalism and Class Struggle in the American Century* (New York: New York University Press), p.167; see also Sales, *From Civil Rights to Black Liberation*, pp.127-131; Branch's *Pillar of Fire*.

16. Mary L. Dudziak, *Cold War Civil Rights: Race and the Image of American Democracy* (Princeton: Princeton University Press, 2000), pp. 220-6.

17. Breitman, George , ed., *Malcolm X Speaks: Selected Speeches and Statements* (New York: Grove Weidenfeld, 1965), pp. 6-12.

18. Ibid., pp. 38-39.

19. Ibid., p. 9.

20. Thomas L. Blair, *Retreat to the Ghetto: The End of a Dream?* (New York: Hill and Wang, 1977), p.74.

21. Ibid., p. 88.

22. Muse, *The American Negro Revolution*, pp. 204-5.

23. Gerald Horne, *Fire This Time: The Watts Uprising and 1960s* (New York: Da Capo, 1997), p. 3.

24. Muse, *The American Negro Revolution*, p.206,; Horne cites property damages as "estimated at $200 million," p. 3; The McCone Commission's figure is $40,000,000. For the latter, go to www.usc.edu/isd/archives/cityinstress/mccone/part3.html.

25. Garrow, *Bearing the Cross*, p. 435.

26. Ibid., p.436.

27. Horne, *Fire This Time*, p. 183.

28. Ibid., p.183.

29. Ibid., p.183.

30. Garrow, *Bearing the Cross*, p.439.

31. Ibid., p. 539; see also Andrew Kopkind, *Thirty Years' Wars: Dispatches and Diversions of a Radical Journalist, 1965–1994* (London: Verso, 1995), p. 89.

32. Branch, *Parting the Waters*, p. 635.

33. Ibid., 479; see also Garrow, *Bearing the Cross*, p. 162., and Breitman, *Malcolm X Speaks*, p.15.

34. Garrow, *Bearing the Cross*, p. 490.

35. Kopkind, *Thirty Years' Wars*, p. 92.

36. Gerald Horne, *Black and Red: W. E. B. Du Bois and the Afro-American Response to the Cold War* (Albany, 1996)

37. Branch, *Parting the Waters*, pp. 478-479.

38. Stokely Carnichael, *Ready for Revolution: The Life and Struggles of Stokely Carmichael* [Kwame Ture] (New York: Simon and Schuster, 2003), p. 224.

39. See Clayborne Carson, *In Struggle: SNCC and the Black Awakening of the 1960s* (Cambridge: Harvard Univeristy Press, 1981), Chapters 14 and 18; see also James Forman's *The Making of Black Revolutionaries* (Seattle: University of Washington Press, 2000) and Robert L. Allen's *Black Awakening in Capitalist America* (Trenton: Africa World Press, 1992).

40. Carnichael, *Ready for Revolution*, pp.662-663.

41. Frantz Fanon, *The Wretched of the Earth* (New York: Grove Press, 1963), p. 94

42. Dudziak, *Cold War Civil Rights*, p. 226.

43. Carson, *In Struggle*, p. 287.

44. Ibid., p. 222.

45. Scot Brown, *Fighting For US: Maulana Karenga, the US Organization, and Black Cultural Nationalism* (New York: New York University Press, 2003), p. 70.

46. John Hope Franklin, *From Slavery to Freedom* (New York: Vintage, 1969), p.59.

47. Smith, *We Have No Leaders*, p. 75.

48. Ibid., p.75.

49. For a history of Baraka's metamorphosis see Watts' *Amiri Baraka: The Politics and Art of a Black Intellectual*. For a different and more sympathetic view of Baraka and the nationalist agenda see Komozi Woodward's *A Nation within a Nation: Amiri Baraka (Le Roi Jones) and Black Power Politics* (Chapel Hill: The University of North Carolina Press, 1999)

50. West, *Prophesy Deliverance!*, p. 23.

51. Paul Krugman, "The Great Tax-Cut Con," *New York Times Magazine*, September 14, 2003, pp. 56-57.

52. Robert E. Weems, Jr., "Out of the Shadows: Business Enterprise and African American Historiography," *Business and Economic History*, vol. 26, no 1, Fall 1997, pp. 200- 212; see also Weems's *Desegregating the Dollar: African American Consumerism in the Twentieth Century* (New York: New York University, 1998)

53. Harold Cruse, *Plural But Equal* (New York: Quill, 1987), p. 75.

54. Ibid., p.76.

55. Cruse, *Crisis of the Negro Intellectual*, p. 86.

CHAPTER FOUR: THE POLITICS AND ECONOMICS OF SOUL POWER, OR "GOOD-FOOT" CAPITALISM AND BLACK AMERICA'S RHYTHM NATION

1. Raymond Williams, *Marxism and Literature* (Oxford: Oxford University Press, 1977), pp.131-132.

2. Thomas Barry, "The Importance of Being Mr. James Brown," *Look*, February 18, 1969. See also Geoff Brown, *James Brown: Doin' It To Death; A Biography*, (London: Omnibus Press, 1996); James Brown with Bruce Tucker, *James Brown: The Godfather of Soul*, (New York: Macmillian, 1986); Cynthia Rose, *Living in America: The Soul Saga of James Brown*, (London: Serpent's Tail, 1990).

3. Ibid., Barry, "Importance of Being Mr. James Brown."

4. Ibid.

5. Ibid.

6. Ibid.

7. Du Bois, *Dusk of Dawn*, p. 198.

8. Alan Hughes, "Hip Hop Economy from New York To Nepal," *Black Enterprise*, May 2002.

9. Cruse, *Crisis*, p. 310.

10. Cruse, *Crisis*, chapters "Mass Media and Cultural Democracy" pp. 64-95 and "Cultural Leadership pp. 96-111.

11. Robert L. Allen's *Black Awakening in Capitalist America* (Trenton: Africa World Press, 1992), p. 229.

12. Ibid., p. 177.

13. Ibid., p. 178.

14. Cruse, p. 328.

15. Allen, pp., 13, 118.

16. Barry, "The Importance of Being Mr. James Brown."

17. Harvard Report ("A Study of the Soul Music Environment, Prepared for Columbia Records Group"), May 11, 1972, p. 18.

18. Rob Bowman, *Soulsville, USA: The Story of Stax Records* (New York: Schirmer Books, 1997),p. 251.

19. Nelson George, *The Death of Rhythm & Blues* (New York: Obelisk/E. P. Dutton, 1989), pp. 165-167.

20 Norman Kelley, ed., *Rhythm and Business: The Political Economy of Black Music* (New York: Akashic Books), see Part One: "The Structure of Stealing" and Part Four: "The Politics of the Noise."

21. Michael Roberts, "Papa's Got a Brand New Bag: Big Music's Post-Fordist

Regime and the Role of Independents Music Labels," Norman Kelley, ed., *Rhythm & Business: The Political Economy of Black Music* (New York: Akashic Books, 2002), pp. 24-43.

22. Juliet E. K. Walker, *The History of Black Business in America: Capitalism, Race, Entrepreneurship* (New York: Macmillan, 1998), p. 328.

23. Norman Kelley, Michael Jackson Allegations Hit a Wrong Note," *Newsday*, July 19, 2002, p. A35

24. Norman Kelley, "Notes on the Political Economy of Black Music," Norman Kelley, ed., *Rhythm & Business: The Political Economy of Black Music* (New York: Akashic Books, 2002), p. 10.

25. Cruse, p. 332.

26. Cruse, p. 65.

Chapter Five: Notes on the Niggarati, or, Why Dead White Men Still Rule

1 E. Franklin Frazier, *E. Franklin Frazier on Race Relations: Selected Writings*, edited by G. Franklin Edwards (Chicago: University of Chicago Press, 1968), p. 274.

2 Cruse, p. 65.

3 Manning Marable, "The Politics of Hip Hop," Urban Think Tank, www.urbanthinktank./politicshiphop.cfm; see also Marable's *Along the Colorline*.

4 Manning Marable, *How Capitalism Underdeveloped Black America* (Cambridge: South End Press, 2000), p. 167.

5. Norman Kelley, "Blacked Out: Hip-Hop and R&B Artists MIA in Music Industry Struggle," *The Village Voice*, June 11, 2002, pp. 47, 48, 51.

6. bell hooks, "Hardcore Honey", Interview of Lil' Kim, *Paper Magazine*, April 1997.

7. See Thulani Davis' "Spinning Race at Harvard," *The Village Voice*, January 22, 2002, and Martin Kilson's "Master of the Intellectual Dodge: A Reply to Henry Louis Gates," *West Africa Review* [vol. 1, no. 2 [?] 2000.

8. Christopher Lasch, *The Revolt of the Elites and the Betrayal Democracy* (New York: W.W. Norton, 1995), Chapter 2, pp. 25-49.

9. Henry Louis Gates, Jr. "Powell and the Black Elite," *The New Yorker*, September 25, 1995.

10. Manning Marable, "Black Intellectuals in Conflict," *New Politics*, Summer 1995, Vol. 5, No.3, p. 39.

11. Adolph Reed, "What Are the Drums, Booker?: The Curious Role of the Black Intellectual," *Class Notes* (New York: The New Press, 2000), pp. 77-90 (This article originally appeared in *The Village Voice*, April 11, 1995); See also Leon Wieseltier, "All and Nothing at All: The Unreal world of Cornel West," *The New Republic*, March 6, 1995, pp. 31-36.

12. Ibid., p. 39.

13. David Rieff, "Multiculturalism's Silent Partner," *Harper's Magazine*, August 1993, pp. 62-72.

14. David Lehman, *Sign of the Times* (New York: Poseidon Press, 1991), pp. 83-84.

15. Haruki Murakami, *The Wind-up Bird Chronicle* (New York: Vintage International, 1998), pp. 76-77.

16. Frazier, p. 271.

17. Emily Eakin, "The Latest Theory Is That Theory Doesn't Matter," *The New York Times*, April 19, 2003; www.nytimes.com/2003/04/19/arts/19CRIT.html.

18. Ibid.

19. Ibid.

20. Ibid.

21. Ibid.

22. Ibid.

23. Alexander Star, "Academic all-stars debate war, politics, and the anxiety of non-influence," *The Boston Globe*, April 20, 2003, www.boston.com/dailyglobe2/110/focus/ Crisis_ theory +.shtml.

24. See Adolph Reed's trenchant dissection of Gates's agenda and politics in "Henry Louis Gates Jr.: From Signifying Monkey to Vital Center," *W. E. B. Du Bois and American Political Thought* (New York: Oxford University Press,1997), pp. 138-162.

25. Martin Kilson, Master of the Intellectual Dodge: A Reply to Henry Louis Gates," *West Africa Review*, [vol. 1, No. 2 [?], 2000.

26. For a possible Israeli/Likud Party connection, see Joseph Cirincione, "Origins of Regime Change in Iraq," Proliferation Brief, Volume 6, Number 5, Wednesday, March 19, 2003; *www.ceip.org/files/nonprolif/templates/Publications.asp? p=8&PublicationID=1214*.

27. Jacob Weisberg, "The Cult of Leo Struass," *Newsweek*, August 3, 1987, p. 61.

28. Brent Staples, "Undemocratic Vistas: The Sinister Vogue of Leo Strauss," *The New York Times*, November 28, 1994, p. A16.

29. Shadia B. Drury, *Leo Struass and the American Right* (New York: St. Martin's

Press, 1997), p. 2. See also Drury's other book on Struass, *The Political Ideas of Leo Strauss* (New York: St. Martin's Press, 1988).

30. Karl Jahn, " Leo Strauss and the Straussarians," *The American Nationalist*, http://home.earthlink.net/~karljahn/index.htm.

31. Early in the spring of 1996, *Social Text* published an essay suggesting a link between quantum mechanics and post-modernism by Professor Alan Sokal, a physicist at New York University. On the day of publication Sokal announced in *Lingua Franca* that the article had in fact been a hoax. In "Transgressing the Boundaries: Toward a Transformative Hermeneutics of Quantum Gravity," Spring/Summer 1996 issue of *Social Text*, Sokal engaged in one of the first direct attacks in the disciplines of cultural studies and critical theory in a major academic journal. This hood-winking was made possible by the fact that Sokal used the sort of cul-tural studies lexicon—"interrogate," "problematize," etc.—that initiates use. Suckered, they fell for it hook, line, and sinker.

CHAPTER SIX: THE POLITICS OF ELECTORAL INSTABILITY

1. Ron Walters, "Blacks and the Democratic Party," *The Nation*, December 16, 2002, p. 18.

2. Ibid., p. 18.

3. Ibid., p. 19.

4. Ibid., p. 19.

5. Ibid., p. 20.

6. Micah Sifry, *Spoiling for a Fight: Third Party Politics in America* (New York: Rout-ledge, 2002), p. 6.

7. Jake Tapper, "And Then There Were None: J.C. Watts and the Lonely Plight of the Black Republican," *Washington Post National Weekly Edition*, January 13-19, 2003, p. 9.

8. Ibid., p. 9.

9. Sifry, *Spoiling for a Fight*, p. 49.

10. Tapper, "And Then There Were None," p. 9.

11. Diana Jean Schomo, "U. S. Schools Turn More Segregated, a Study Finds," *New York Times*, July 20, 2001.

12. Jodi Wilogren, "Young Blacks Turn To School Vouchers As Civil Rights Issues," *New York Times*, October 9, 2000, pp. A1, A16.

13. Ibid. A16.

14. Michael Leo Owens, "Why Blacks Support Vouchers," *New York Times*, February 26, 2002, p. A25.

15. Ibid., p.A25.

16. Sifry, p. 10.

17. Adam Nagourney and Carl Hulse, "Bush Rebukes Lott Over Remarks on Thurmond," *New York Times*, December 13, 2002, p. A36.

18. Frances Fox Piven and Richard A. Cloward, *Poor People's Movement: How They Succeed, How They Fail* (New York: Vintage, 1979), p. 254.

19. Thulani Davis, "Al vs. the Dems: Presidential Candidate Sharpton Goes After His Party," *The Village Voice*, February 26–March 4, 2003, p. 49.

BIBLIOGRAPHY

BOOKS

Allen, Robert L., *Black Awakening in Capitalist America*, Trenton: Africa World Press, 1992.

Blair, Thomas, *Retreat to the Ghetto: End of the Dream?*, New York: Hill and Wang, 1977.

Blumenthal, Sidney, *The Rise of a Counter-Establishment: From Conservative Ideology to Political Power*, New York: Times Books, 1986.

Branch, Taylor, *Parting the Waters: America in the King Years, 1954-1963*, New York: Simon and Schuster, 1988.

—*Pillar of Fire: America in the King Years, 1963-1965*, New York: Simon and Schuster, 1998.

Breitman, George, ed., *Malcolm X Speaks: Selected Speeches and Statements*. New York: Grove Weidenfeld, 1965.

Brown, Michael K., et al., *Whitewashing Race: The Myth of a Colorblind Society*, Berkeley: University of California, 2003.

Brown, Scot, *Fighting For US: Maulana Karenga, the US Organization, and Black Cultural Nationalism*, New York: New York University Press, 2003.

Bush, Rod *We Are Not What We Seem: Black Nationalism and Class Struggle in the American Century*, New York: New York University Press, 1999.

Carmichael, Stokely (Kwame Ture) and Charles V. Hamilton, *Black Power: The Politics of Liberation in America*, New York: Vintage, 1967.

Carmichael, Stokely (Kwame Ture), *Ready for Revolution*, New York: Simon and Schuster (Scribner), 2003.

Carson, Clayborne. *In Struggle: SNCC and the Black Awakening of the 1960s*. Cambridge: Harvard University Press, 1981.

Carter, Dan T., *The Politics of Rage: George Wallace, the Origins of the New Conservatism, and the Transformation of American Politics*, New York: Simon & Schuster, 1995.

—*From George Wallace to New Gingrich: Race in the Conservative Counterrevolution, 1963–1994*, Baton Rouge: Louisiana State University Press, 1996.

Clegg, Claude Andrew, *An Original Man: The Life and Times of Elijah Muhammad*, New York: St. Martin's Press, 1997.

Coser, Lewis, *Men of Ideas*, New York: Free Press, 1965.

Cruse, Harold, *The Crisis of the Negro Intellectual*, New York: Quill, 1967.

—*Plural But Equal: A Critical Study of Blacks and Minorities and America Plural Society*, New York: Quill, 1987.

Dent, Gina, ed., *Black Popular Culture: a project by Michele Wallace*, Seattle: Bay Press, 1992.

Dittmer, John, *Local People: The Struggle for Civil Rights in Mississippi*, Urbana: University of Illinois Press, 1995.

Dudziak, Mary L., *Cold War Civil Rights: Race and the Image of American Democracy*. Princeton: Princeton University Press, 2000.

DuBois, W.E.B, *Dusk of Dawn: An Essay Toward an Autobiography of Race*, New Brunswick: Transaction Publishers, 1995.

—*Black Reconstruction in America, 1860-1880*, Cleveland: Meridian Books, 1968.

—*The Souls of Black Folk*, New York: Gramercy Books, 1994

Drury, Shadia B. *Leo Struass and the American Right*, New York: St. Martin's Press, 1997.

Edwards, G. Franklin, ed., *E. Franklin Frazier on Race Relations: Selected Writings*, Chicago: University of Chicago Press, 1968.

Fanon, Frantz, *The Wretched of the Earth*, New York: Grove Press, 1963.

Forman, James, *The Making of Black Revolutionaries*, Seattle: University of Washington Press, 2000.

Franklin, John Hope, *From Slavery to Freedom*, New York: Vintage, 1969.

Frazier, E. Franklin, *Black Bourgeosie*, New York: MacMillian Publishing Co., 1957.

Garrow, David, *Bearing the Cross: Martin Luther King, Jr. and the Southern Christian Leadership Conference*. London: Vintage, 1986.

Genovese, Eugene D., *Roll Jordan, Roll: The Slaves the World Made*, New York, Random House, 1976.

George, Nelson, *The Death of Rhythm & Blues*, New York: Obelisk/E. P. Dutton, 1989.

Gerth, H. H. and C Wright Mills, eds., *From Max Weber: Essays in Sociology*, New York: Oxford University Press, 1972.

Gitlin, Todd, *The Whole World is Watching: Mass Media in the Making and Unmaking of the New Left*, Berkeley: University of California Press, 1980.

Guillory, Monique and Richard Green, eds., *Soul: Black Power, Politics and Pleasure*, New York, New York University Press: 1998.

Hamilton, Charles, *Adam Clayton Powell: The Political Biography of an American Dilemma*. New York: Atheneum, 1991.

Horne, Gerald. *Fire This Time: The Watts Uprising and the 1960s* New York: Da Capo, 1997.

Jacoby, Russell, *The Last Intellectuals: American Culture in the Age of Academe*, New York: Farrar, Straus and Giroux, 1987.

Johnson, Ollie A., III, and Karin L. Stanford, eds., *Black Political Organizations in the Post-Civil Rights Era*, New Brunswick: Rutgers University Press, 2002.

Kelley, Norman, ed., *Rhythm and Business: The Political Economy of Black Music*, New York: Akashic Books, 2002.

King, Martin Luther, *Where Do We Go From Here: Chaos or Community?*, Boston: Beacon, 1967.

Kopkind, Andrew, *Thirty Years' War: Dispatches and Diversions of a Radical Journalist, 1965–1994*. London: Verso, 1995.

Lasch, Christopher, *The Revolt of the Elite and the Betrayal of America*, New York: W.W. Norton, 1995.

Lind, Michael, *The Next American Nation*, New York: Free Press, 1995.

Lehman, David, *Sign of the Times*, New York: Poseidon Press, 1991).

Logan, Rayford, W., *The Betrayal of the Negro*, London: Collier Books, 1970.

Malcolm X, *The Autobiography of Malcolm X*, New York: Grove Press, 1964.

Marable, Manning, *How Capitalism Underdeveloped Black America*, Cambridge: South End Press, 2000.

Murakami, Haruki , *The Wind-up Bird Chronicle*, New York: Vintage International, 1998.

Muse, Benjamin, *The American Negro Revolution: From Nonviolence to Black Power*, New York: Citadel Press, 1970.

Piven, Frances Fox and Richard Cloward, *Poor People's Movement: How They Succeed, How They Fail*, New York: Vintage, 1979.

Postman, Neil, *Amusing Ourselves to Death: Public Discourse in the Age of Show Business*, New York: Viking Penguin, 1985.

Reed, Adolph, Jr., *Class Notes: Posing as Politics and Other Thoughts on the American Scene*, New York: The New Press, 2000.

—*Stirrings in the Jug: Black Politics in the Post-Segregation Era*. Minneapolis, University of Minnesota Press, 1999.

—*W.E.B. DuBois and American Political Thought: Fabianism and the Color Line.* New York: Oxford University Press, 1997.

—*The Jesse Jackson Phenomenon*, New Haven: Yale University Press, 1986.

Reed, Ishmael, *Airing Dirty Laundry*, Reading: Addison-Wesley, 1993.

Roberts, Michael, "Papa's Got a Brand New Bag: Big Music's Post-Fordist Regime and the Role of Independents Music Labels," Norman Kelley, ed., *Rhythm & Business: The Political Economy of Black Music*, New York: Akashic Books, 2002.

Rustin, Bayard, *Down the Line: The Collected Writings of Bayard Rustin.* Chicago: Quadrangle Books, 1971.

Sifry, Micah *Spoiling for a Fight: Third Party Politics in America*, New York: Routledge, 2002.

Smith, Robert C. *We Have No Leaders: African Americans in the Post Civil Rights Era.* Albany: SUNY Press, 1996.

Stefancic, Jean and Robert Delagado, *No Mercy: How Conservative Think Tanks and Foundations Changed America's Social Agenda.* Philadelphia: Temple University Press, 1998.

Timmerman, Kenneth R., *Shakedown: Exposing the Real Jesse Jackson*, Washington, D. C.: Regnery Publishing, Inc., 2002.

Walker, Juliet E. K., *The History of Black Business in America: Capitalism, Race, Entrepreneurship*, New York: Macmillian, 1998.

Walters, Ronald V. and Robert C. Smith, *African American Leadership*, Albany: SUNY Press, 1999.

Watts, Jerry Gafio, *Amiri Baraka: The Politics and Art of a Black Intellectual.* New York: New York University, 20001.

Weems, Robert E., *Desegregating the Dollar: African American Consumerism in the Twentieth Century.* New York: New York University Press, 1998.

West, Cornel, *Prophesy Deliverance: Afro-American Revolutionary Christianity*, Philadelphia: The Westminster Press, 1982.

Williams, Raymond, *Marxism and Literature*, Oxford: Oxford University Press, 1977.

Wilson, William Julius, *The Declining Significance of Race*, Chicago: University of Chicago, 1978.

Woodward, C. Vann, *The Strange Career of Jim Crow*, New York: Oxford University Press, 1966.

Woodward, Komozi, *A Nation with in a Nation: Amiri Baraka (Le Roi Jones) and Black Power Politics*, Chapel Hill: The University of North Carolina Press, 1999.

PERIODICALS (NEWSPAPERS, MAGAZINES, JOURNALS)

Barry, Thomas, "The Importance of Being Mr. James Brown," *Look* magazine, February 18, 1969.

Cockburn, Alexander, "The Book of Numbers," *New York Press*, January 21-27, 2001, p. 11.

Crouch, Stanley, "Rev. Al is Going for a Lot More Than Glory," *New York Daily News*, Dec. 18, 2003.

Davis, Thulani "Al vs. the Dems: Presidential Candidate Sharpton Goes After His Party," *The Village Voice*, February 26 - March 4, 2003.

——"Spinning Race at Harvard," *The Village Voice*, January 22, 2002.

Gates, Henry Louis, Jr. "Hating Hillary," *The New Yorker*, February 26 & March 4, 1996.

——"Powell and the Black Elite," The New Yorker, September 25, 1995.

hooks, bell, "Hardcore Honey"(Interview of Lil' Kim), *Paper Magazine*, April 1997.

Hughes, Alan, "Hip Hop Economy from New York to Nepal," *Black Enterprise*, May 2002.

Kelley, Norman, "Memoirs of a Revolutionist," *The Nation*, December 8, 2003.*

——"HNIC #3: Al Sharpton and the Slow Death of Black Politics," *New York Press*, February 19-25, 2003. *

——"The Neverland Music Summit," *The Village Voice*, July 23, 2002. *

——"Keepin' It Real?: Music Revolution or a King on the Loose," *The Village Voice*, July 16, 2002.*

——"Blacked Out: Hip-Hop and R&B Artists MIA in Music Industry Struggle," *The Village Voice*, June 11, 2002

——"Black Cultural Criticism Inc.," *New York Press*, April 17-23, 2002. *

——"Black Politics in the Age of Clinton," *New York Press*, July 19-25, 2000. *

——"Notes on the Niggerati," *New Politics*, Winter 1996.*

Kilson, Martin "The Weakness of Black Politics," *Dissent*, Fall 1987.

——"Master of the Intellectual Dodge: A Reply to Henry Louis Gates," *West Africa Review* [vol. 1, no. 2 [?] 2000.

Marable, Manning, "Black Intellectuals in Conflict," *New Politics*, Summer 1995, Vol. 5, No.3

Monroe, Sylvester, "Cornel Matters," *Emerge*, September 1996.

Nagourney, Adam and Carl Hulse, "Bush Rebukes Lott Over Remarks on Thurmond," *New York Times*, December 16, 2002.

Novak, Robert, "How Farrakhan Could Energize the Republican Party," *New York Post*, March 6, 1997.

Owens, Michael Leo, "Why Blacks Support Vouchers," *New York Times*, February 26, 2002.

Reed, Adolph, "Steele Trap," *The Nation*, March 4, 1991.

Rieff, David, "Multiculturalism's Silent Partner," *Harper's Magazine*, August 1993.

Schomo, Diana Jean, "U. S. Schools Turn More Segregated, a Study Finds," *New York Times*, July 20, 2001.

Shatz, Adam, "Glenn Loury's About Face," *New York Time Magazine*, January 20, 2002.

Sokal, Alan, "Transgressing the Boundaries: Toward a Transformative Hermeneutics of Quantum Gravity," *Social Text*, Spring/Summer 1996.

Staples, Brent, "Undemocratic Vistas: The Sinister Vogue of Leo Strauss, *The New York Times*, November 28, 1994.

Toler, Deborah, "Black Conservatives," *The Public Eye*, Somerville: Political Research Associates, 1993.

Tapper, Jake, "And Then There Were None: J.C. Watts and the Lonely Plight of the Black Republican," *Washington Post National Weekly Edition*, January 13-19, 2003.

Walters, Ron, "Blacks and the Democratic Party," *The Nation*, December 16, 2002.

Weems, Robert E., "Out of the Shadows: Business Enterprise and African American Historiography," *Business and Economic History*, 26; 1, Fall 1997.

Weisberg, Jacob, "The Cult of Leo Strauss," *Newsweek*, August 3, 1987.

Wieseltier, Leon, "All and Nothing at All: The Unreal World of Cornel West," *The New Republic*, March 6, 1995.

Wilogren, Jodi, "Young Blacks Turn To School Vouchers As Civil Rights Issues," *New York Times*, October 9, 2000.

REPORTS

Covington, Sally, "Moving A Public Policy Agenda: The Strategic Philanthropy of Conservative Foundations." Washington, DC: National Committee for Responsive Philanthropy, 1997.

"Harvard Report," (Study of the Soul Music Environment, Prepared for CBS Records) May 11, 1972.

"Report of the National Advisory Commission on Civil Disorders," March 1, 1968 ("The Kerner Commission")

ON-LINE ARTICLES

Associated Press, www.msnbc.com/news/854722.asp?0cv=CB10, January 3, 2003.

Cirincione, Joseph "Origins of Regime Change in Iraq," 20Proliferation Brief, Volume 6, Number 5, Wednesday, March 19, 2003;*www.ceip.org/files/ nonprolif/templates/Publications.asp?p=8&PublicationID=1214*.

Clingman , James E, "Turning 'Spending Weakness' Into Power," www.sacobserver.com/business/commentary/091603/black_spending_ weakness.shtml.

Eakin, Emily, "The Latest Theory Is That Theory Doesn't Matter," *The New York Times*, April 19, 2003; www.nytimes.com/2003/04/19/arts/19CRIT.html.

Jahn, Karl, "Leo Strauss and the Straussarians," The American Nationalist, http://home.earthlink.net/~karljahn/index.htm.

Marable, Manning "The Politics of Hip Hop," Urban Think Tank, www.urbanthinktank./politicshiphop.cfm.

Star, Alexander, "Academic all-stars debate war, politics, and the anxiety of non-influence," *The Boston Globe*, April 20, 2003, www.boston.com/daily-globe2/110/focus/ Crisis_theory+.shtml.

MISCELLANEOUS

Brian Lehrer Show, WNYC radio (audio file), www.wnyc.org/shows/ bl/episodes/12112003.

*A NOTE TO THE READERS:

Portions of this book appeared in one form or another over the years in such publications as the *Village Voice*, *New York Press*, *New Politics* and *the Nation*. The introduction includes "Black Politics in the Age of Clinton"; Chapter One originally appeared as "HNIC #3: Al Sharpton and the Slow Death of Black Politics," and includes passages from "The Neverland Music Summit," and "Keepin' It Real?: Music Revolution or a King on the Loose." Chapter Three has a tad from "Memoirs of a Revolutionist." Chapter Five includes portions of "Black Cultural Criticism, Inc." as well as "Notes on the Niggarti." Finally, the genesis of this book began with an article, *Disappearing Act: The Decline of Black Leadership*, that was published in *The Bedford-Stuyvesant Current*, Winter 1997.

INDEX

affirmative action programs,
57-58, 68, 79, 154
African American politics. *See*
black politics
Afrocentrism, 45-46, 109
Aid to Families with Dependent
Children (AFDC), 68
Allen, Robert, 126-27, 128-29
American society: as anti-intel-
lectual, 6; black politics and,
48-49
Amusing Ourselves to Death
(Postman), 2
Asante, Molefi Kete, 45

Baraka, Amiri, 110, 111, 129
Barry, Thomas, 120
Bhabha, Homi, 156
black America: bifurcation of,
58-59; rise and fall of, 6-7
*Black Awakening in Capitalist
America* (Allen), 126-27
Black Bourgeoisie (Frazier), 5
black capitalism, 141; *See also*
economic development
black churches, 5-6
black community, bifurcation
of, 58-59

black conservatives, 8, 66-70
Brooker T. Washington
and, 24-25
Bush administration and, 25
Farrakhan and, 47
black economy. *See* economic
development
black freedom movement. *See*
Black Power nationalism;
civil right movement
black gender gap, 197-98
black intellectuals/intellectu-
alism: conservative, 8, 24-25,
47, 66-70
current state of, 2-3
hip-hop music and, 139-44
lack of economic theory
by, 135-36
market, 2-4, 6-7, 67, 140-45
as niggarati, 139, 147-55
obsession of, with
celebrity, 2-6, 8-9
as pop stars, 2; in post-civil
rights era, 70-71
public, 137-42
black leaders/leadership:
See also black politics; *specific
persons*
bifurcation of, 58-59

charismatic nature of, 22-24, 43

corruptness of, 16-17

disappearance of, 7-19

failures of, 152-53, 183-87

female, 197-98

inability of, to mobilize voters, 112

post-civil rights era, 78-82

symbolic nature of, 30

black liberation, 93

black middle class, 127-28

black music

cultural criticism of, 139-44

economic potential of, 113, 115, 118-25, 131

Harvard Report on, 130

hip hop, 36, 59, 60, 118, 124, 131-32, 135, 139-44

impact of, on American society, 127-29

neo-colonization of, 129-36

profits from, for music industry, 130-33, 135

soul music, 117-18

Black Music Association (BMA), 130-31

black nationalism, political philosophy of, 95-96

black orthodoxy, 45-46, 56, 59, 109

Black Panther Party, 60, 105, 107, 111

black politics: See also black leaders/leadership

American society and, 48-49;

black conservatives and, 8-9

charismatic nature of, 22-24, 43

during Clinton years, 12-13

Congressional Black Caucus and, 11, 37, 55, 60-61, 183

demobilization of, 51-52

failures of, 11-19

media and, 40-41

orientation of, 72-74

strategic non-voting and, 171-76, 185-92

symbolic nature of, 9-10, 13; timidity in, 37-38

weakness of, in sustaining institutions, 22-23, 102

Black Popular Culture (Wallace), 142

black poverty: See also economic development

reasons for, 81

Black Power (Carmichael), 105-6

Black Power nationalism, 53, 56 See also civil rights movement; connotations of, 87-88

failures of, 104-9

fragmenting of civil rights movement and, 83-89

King and, 86-88

legacies of, 94, 109

Malcolm X and, 89-97

rise and fall of, 102-15

SNCC and, 103-8
subjective fortification and, 94
Third World colonialism and, 106-9
violence and, 105, 107-8
Watts riots and, 97-100
black progress, reaction to, 70
Black Radical Congress, 113
black studies, 71
black theology, 3, 4-6
black voters: *See also* black politics
Democratic Party and, 17, 37-38, 63-64, 76-78, 103, 167-76, 182, 190-91
Republican Party and, 17, 64-65, 174-75
Bork, Robert, 61
Bositis, David, 30, 31
Branch, Taylor, 70
Braun, Carol Moseley, 39
Brown, H. Rap, 105, 121
Brown, James, 115;
as black leader, 121, 124-25, 129
commercial success of 120, 122-23
cultural apparatus and, 125-29
decline of, 133
double consciousness of, 121-22
economic nationalism of, 118-25

on education, 120-21, 124-25
legacy of, 133-34
soul music and, 117-18
Bush administration, 60-61
Byrd Amendment, 60

Calhoun-Brown, Allison, 6
Carmichael, Stokely, 83-84, 86-87, 103, 104, 105-6, 111, 121
Carson, Clayborne, 108
Carter, Jimmy, 110-11, 182
CBC. *See* Congressional Black Caucus
charismatic leaders, 22-24, 43; *See also specific leaders*
Chomsky, Noam, 156, 157
Christianity, racism and, 3-5
Cisneros, Henry, 199
Civil Rights Act (1964), 54
civil rights legislation, 56-58, 73
civil rights movement:
See also Black Power nationalism
black economic development and, 61-63
as crisis politics, 180-82;
Democratic Party and, 73
economic justice and, 18, 54, 73-77, 78-79
fragmenting of, 83-89, 100-2
institutionalization of, 59-60
leading organizations of, 52-53, 84-85

main goals of, 53, 84-85;
Malcolm X and, 89-97
Martin Luther King and,
54-55, 75, 84, 86-88
political incorporation of,
51-52, 56-57
post-King, 56
Republican Party and, 38
results of, 147
rise and fall of, 6-7
Watts riots and, 97-100
Clegg, Claude Andrew, 90, 91
Clinton, Bill
black voters and, 12-13
as "first black President,"
14-15
Lewinsky affair of, 11-13
Massa complex and, 28-29
record of, 63
welfare reform by, 68-69
Clinton, Hillary, 16
COINTELPRO, 56
Confederate flag issue, 16
Congressional Black Caucus
(CBC), 11, 37, 55, 60-61, 183
Congress of Racial Equality
(CORE), 52-53, 88
conservative movement
black, 8, 24-25, 47, 66-70
Leo Strauss and, 158-63,
164-65
power of, 77
Contents of Our Character, The
(Steele), 65-66

Contract with America, 11, 46
Council for United Civil Rights
Leadership, 100-1
Council of Federated
Organizations (COFO),
100-1
Crisis of the Negro Intellectual, The
(Cruse), 125-29
crisis politics, 179-82
Crouch, Stanley, 34-35
Cruse, Harold, 14, 81, 114-15,
125-29, 136, 140
cultural apparatus, 125-29
cultural criticism, 138-46
Currier, Stephen, 100

Dean, Howard, 36
de Man, Paul, 149
Democratic Leadership
Council, 112
Democratic Party
black voters, 17
black voters and, 37-38,
63-64, 76-78, 103, 167-76,
182, 190-91
civil rights movement
and, 73
reorganization of
Southern, 76
Sharpton's campaign and,
31-32
Dinkins, David N., 42
Drury, Shadia B., 159

Du Bois, W.E.B., 21, 62, 70, 78, 79-80, 102, 123-24, 154-55
Dyson, Michael Eric, 7, 23, 142

economic development, 17-18, 61-63, 78-80, 113-14, 153-54
economic disparity, 17-18
economic justice, 73-77, 78-79
economic nationalism, James Brown and, 118-25
economic potential, of black music, 113, 115, 118-25, 131
education issues, 64-65, 168, 176-79, 187-89
Elders, Joycelyn, 15
electoral instability, 172-76; See also strategic non-voting
Evans, Robert, 47

Fair Employment Practices Commission (FEPC), 74
faith-based initiatives, 64-65
Fanon, Frantz, 17, 106
Farrakhan, Louis, 9, 13, 19, 45-48, 50-51, 113, 155
Fish, Stanley, 156
Folsom, Jim, 17
Frazier, E. Franklin, 5, 139

Garrow, David, 87
Garvey, Marcus, 26

Gates, Henry Louis, Jr., 12, 147, 148-49, 153, 156-57
Genovese, Eugene, 48
Gilman, Sander L., 156
Gitlin, Todd, 40
Gordy, Berry, 128, 129, 131-32
Gore, Al, 14-15, 190-91
Guinier, Lani, 15

Ham, curse of, 4
Head Negro in Charge Syndrome (HNICS), 7-8
    current version of, 29
    examples of, 9-10
    roots of, 21
    Sharpton and, 32
Hill, Anita, 12
hip-hop music, 36, 59, 60, 118, 124, 131-32, 135, 139-44; See also black music
Hip-Hop Summit Action Network (HSAN), 35
hooks, bell, 142-44
Horne, Gerald, 99

incarceration rate, 63
inner cities, 59, 60, 101, 153-54
intellectuals/intellectualism. See black intellectuals/intellectualism
Iraq war, 158, 163
Israel, 162

Jackson, Jesse, 9-10, 13-14, 18-19, 31, 42, 112, 169
Jackson, Michael, 32-34, 133
Jacoby, Russell, 2
Jahn, Karl, 160-61
Joint Center for Political and Economic Studies, 78
journals, public affairs, 71-72

Karenga, Maulana Ron, 45, 109
Kennedy administration, 28, 74, 75, 102-3, 180
Kilson, Martin, 42
King, Martin Luther, Jr.
    civil rights movement and, 52, 54-55, 75, 84, 86-88
    Jesse Jackson and, 19
    march against fear and, 83-84, 87-88
    Watts riots and, 98-100
Klein, Joe, 31
Kopkind, Andrew, 101
Krugman, Paul, 112
Kwanzaa, 45, 109

Last Intellectuals, The (Jacoby), 2
Lehman, David, 149-51
Lewis, John, 11
Lil' Kim, 142-43
Lind, Michael, 16, 58

Logan, Rayford, 70
Lott, Trent, 17, 64
Loury, Glenn, 69
Lynch, Willie, 48

magazines, 71-72
Malcolm X, 48, 89-97, 155
Marable, Manning, 14, 140-41, 147-49, 153
march against fear, 83-84, 87-88
March on Washington for Jobs and Freedom (1963), 73-77
market intellectuals, 2-4, 6-7, 67, 140-45
Massa complex, 27-29
McAuliffe, Terry, 168-69
media, black politics and, 40-41
Meredith, James, 83
Messiah complex, 26-27
Million Man March, 9, 11, 45, 46-48, 50, 113
Mitchell, W.J.T., 156
Montgomery Bus Boycott, 50
Morrison, Toni, 14
Motown, 131-32, 134
Mottola, Tommy, 33
Muhammad, Ben Chavis, 35
Muhammad, Conrad, 35-36
Muhammad, Elijah, 61, 76, 89, 90-91
Muhammad, Khalid, 13
multiculturalism, 149

Murakami, Haruki, 151-52
music industry. *See* black music

NAACP. *See* National Association for the Advancement of Colored People
National Association for the Advancement of Colored People (NAACP), 50, 52-53, 61-62, 81, 85-88, 101-2, 113-14
national black political directorate, 183-85
National Summit for Fairness in the Recording Industry, 32-35
Nation of Islam, 76
 black identity and, 93-94
 conservatism of, 90
 Elijah Muhammad and, 90-91
 Malcolm X and, 89-97
Neal, Mark Anthony, 35
neoconservatives, 162-63
Niagara Movement (1905), 50
Nicholas V (pope), 4
niggarati, 139, 147-55, 164-65
Nixon, Richard, 126
noneconomic liberalism, 62, 75, 113-14
Norton, Eleanor Holmes, 11

Ogletree, Charles J., 12

police brutality, 42-43
politics
 See also black politics; crisis, 179-82
Poor People's Campaign, 55
post-civil rights era, 56-59, 70, 78-82
Postman, Neil, 2
postmodern princes, 9
Powell, Adam Clayton, Jr., 13, 55-56, 61, 85
Powell, Colin, 25, 147, 175-76
President's Urban Strategy, 199-212
progressive Marxism, 3
Prophesy Deliverance! (West), 3-4, 24
public affairs journals, 71-72
public education, failures of, 16, 176-79, 187-89
public intellectuals, 137-42

Race Matters (West), 2-3, 147
 racial realist writing, 66
racism
 Christianity and, 3-5
 genealogy of modern, 3-4
Randolph, A. Philip, 54, 74, 75
Rangel, Charles, 11, 16
Reagan administration, 38, 60-61, 68, 152-53, 184
Reconstruction, 70

Reed, Adolph, 2, 14, 37-38, 39, 184
reparations movement, 10, 81
Republican Party
    black conservatives and, 69
    black voters and, 17, 64-65, 174-75
    civil rights movement and, 38
    conservative movement and, 77
    cuts in public spending by, 112
    Farrakhan and, 46-47
    neoconservatives and, 163
Rhythm Nation, 129, 129-36
Rice, Condoleezza, 25
Rieff, David, 149
Rivers, Eugene, 137
Roll, Jordan, Roll (Genovese), 48
Roosevelt, Franklin, 74
Rustin, Bayard, 37, 54, 55, 73, 88-89, 105

school vouchers, 177-79, 187-88, 189
SCLC. See Southern Christian Leadership Council
Seelye, Katharine, 15
Shakedown (Timmerman), 19
Shakur, Tupac, 27, 142
Sharpton, Al
    black music and, 32-36
    black voters and, 169
    checkered past of, 39-40
    Cornel West and, 145, 195
    on Democratic Party, 191
    effect of, on black politics, 39
    Jesse Jackson and, 31-32
    lack of strong organizational structure behind, 22-23
    media and, 40-41
    Michael Jackson and, 32-34
    police brutality and, 42-43
    presidential candidacy of, 9-10, 14, 19, 29-43, 193-98
    as symbolic leader, 41-43
Sifry, Micah, 174
Sign of the Times, The (Lehman), 149-51
Simmons, Russell, 35, 46
Sketches of My Culture (West), 144
slavery
    black church and, 5-6
    traditional rationalizations for, 4
Smith, Robert C., 31-32, 56-57, 66-67, 110
SNCC. See Student Nonviolent Coordinating Committee
Soul (Guillory and Green), 142
soul music, 117-18, 130;
    See also black music
Souls of Black Folk, The (Du Bois), 21
Southern Christian Leader-

ship Conference (SCLC), 52-53, 88
Stax Records, 130, 131, 134
Steele, Shelby, 65-66
Stewart, Jim, 130
strategic non-voting, 171-76, 185-92
strategic self-segregation, 79-80
Strauss, Leo, 158-63, 164
Student Nonviolent Coordinating Committee (SNCC), 52-53, 85, 88, 100, 103-8, 106-9
Sumners, Lawrence, 1
symbolic politicians, 9

theory, death of, 155-58
Third World colonialism model, 106-7
Thomas, Clarence, 46
Thurmond, Strom, 17
Timmerman, Kenneth, 19
Ture, Kwame. *See* Carmichael, Stokely
Tuskegee machine, 25
2004 presidential campaign, 193-98

U.S. economy, changing in 1970s, 111-12
United Negro Improvement Association (UNIA), 26
urban poverty, 59, 60, 101,

153-54; *See also* economic development
Voting Rights Act (1965), 54, 55, 97, 110

Walker, Juliet, 132-33
Wallace, Michelle, 142
Walters, Ronald, 66-67, 167-69
Washington, Brooker T., 24-25, 62, 78, 118-19, 120
Watts, Jerry G., 43
Watts riots, 85, 86, 97-100
wealth creation.
    See economic development
Weber, Max, 23
welfare dependency, 81
welfare reform, 68-69
West, Cornel
    on black charismatic authority, 23-24
    black economic development and, 153-54
    black political culture and, 23
    Black Power nationalism and, 111
    as market intellectual, 1-4, 6, 8, 144-45, 147
    on racism, 3-5
    Sharpton and, 145, 195
White, Theodore, 97
Whitewashing Race (Brown et al.), 8-9

Wilkins, Roy, 84, 85

Wilson, William Julius, 70

Wind-up Bird Chronicle, The
(Murakami), 151-52

Wohlstetter, Alfred, 158

Woodward, C. Vann, 70

Wretched of the Earth, The
(Fanon), 106

Young, Whitney, 84